LETTERA ENCICLICA

DEUS CARITAS EST

DEL SOMMO PONTEFICE

BENEDETTO XVI

AI VESCOVI
AI PRESBITERI E AI DIACONI
ALLE PERSONE CONSACRATE
E A TUTTI I FEDELI LAICI

SULL'AMORE CRISTIANO

LIBRERIA EDITRICE VATICANA
CITTÀ DEL VATICANO

V Ristampa 2006

© Copyright 2006 – Libreria Editrice Vaticana – 00120 Città del Vaticano
Tel. 06.698.85003 – Fax 06.698.84716

ISBN 88-209-7786-9

www.libreriaeditricevaticana.com

TIPOGRAFIA VATICANA - 2006

INTRODUZIONE

1. «DIO È AMORE; chi sta nell'amore dimora in Dio e Dio dimora in lui» (*1 Gv* 4, 16). Queste parole della *Prima Lettera di Giovanni* esprimono con singolare chiarezza il centro della fede cristiana: l'immagine cristiana di Dio e anche la conseguente immagine dell'uomo e del suo cammino. Inoltre, in questo stesso versetto, Giovanni ci offre per così dire una formula sintetica dell'esistenza cristiana: «Noi abbiamo riconosciuto l'amore che Dio ha per noi e vi abbiamo creduto».

Abbiamo creduto all'amore di Dio — così il cristiano può esprimere la scelta fondamentale della sua vita. All'inizio dell'essere cristiano non c'è una decisione etica o una grande idea, bensì l'incontro con un avvenimento, con una Persona, che dà alla vita un nuovo orizzonte e con ciò la direzione decisiva. Nel suo Vangelo Giovanni aveva espresso quest'avvenimento con le seguenti parole: «Dio ha tanto amato il mondo da dare il suo Figlio unigenito, perché chiunque crede in lui ... abbia la vita eterna» (3, 16). Con la centralità dell'amore, la fede cristiana ha accolto quello che era il nucleo della fede d'Israele e al contempo ha dato a questo nucleo una nuova profondità e ampiezza. L'Israelita credente, infatti, prega ogni giorno con le parole del *Libro del Deuteronomio*, nelle quali egli sa che è racchiuso il centro della sua esistenza: «Ascolta, Israele: il Signore è il nostro Dio, il Signore è uno solo. Tu amerai il Signore tuo Dio con tutto il cuore, con tutta l'anima e con tutte le forze» (6, 4-5). Gesù ha unito, facendone un unico precetto, il comandamento dell'amore di Dio con quello dell'amore del prossimo, contenuto nel *Libro del Levitico*: «Amerai il tuo prossimo come te stesso» (19, 18; cfr *Mc* 12, 29-31). Siccome Dio ci ha amati per primo (cfr *1 Gv* 4, 10), l'amore adesso non è più solo un «comandamento», ma è la risposta al dono dell'amore, col quale Dio ci viene incontro.

In un mondo in cui al nome di Dio viene a volte collegata la vendetta o perfino il dovere dell'odio e della violenza, questo è un messaggio di grande attualità e di significato molto concreto. Per questo nella mia prima Enciclica desidero parlare dell'amore, del quale Dio ci ricolma e che da noi deve essere comunicato agli altri. Ecco così indicate le due grandi parti di questa Lettera, tra loro profondamente connesse. La prima avrà un'indole più speculativa, visto che in essa vorrei precisare — all'inizio del mio Pontificato — alcuni dati essenziali sull'amore che Dio, in modo misterioso e gratuito, offre all'uomo, insieme all'intrinseco legame di quell'Amore con la realtà dell'amore umano. La seconda parte avrà un carattere più concreto, poiché tratterà dell'esercizio ecclesiale del comandamento dell'amore per il prossimo. L'argomento si presenta assai vasto; una lunga trattazione, tuttavia, eccede lo scopo della presente Enciclica. È mio desiderio insistere su alcuni elementi fondamentali, così da suscitare nel mondo un rinnovato dinamismo di impegno nella risposta umana all'amore divino.

PRIMA PARTE

L'UNITÀ DELL'AMORE NELLA CREAZIONE E NELLA STORIA DELLA SALVEZZA

Un problema di linguaggio

2. L'amore di Dio per noi è questione fondamentale per la vita e pone domande decisive su chi è Dio e chi siamo noi. Al riguardo, ci ostacola innanzitutto un problema di linguaggio. Il termine «amore» è oggi diventato una delle parole più usate ed anche abusate, alla quale annettiamo accezioni del tutto differenti. Anche se il tema di questa Enciclica si concentra sulla questione della comprensione e della prassi dell'amore nella Sacra Scrittura e nella Tradizione della Chiesa, non possiamo semplicemente prescindere dal significato che questa parola possiede nelle varie culture e nel linguaggio odierno.

Ricordiamo in primo luogo il vasto campo semantico della parola «amore»: si parla di amor di patria, di amore per la professione, di amore tra amici, di amore per il lavoro, di amore tra genitori e figli, tra fratelli e familiari, dell'amore per il prossimo e dell'amore per Dio. In tutta questa molteplicità di significati, però, l'amore tra uomo e donna, nel quale corpo e anima concorrono inscindibilmente e all'essere umano si schiude una promessa di felicità che sembra irresistibile, emerge come archetipo di amore per eccellenza, al cui confronto, a prima vista, tutti gli altri tipi di amore sbiadiscono. Sorge allora la domanda: tutte queste forme di amore alla fine si unificano e l'amore, pur in tutta la diversità delle sue manifestazioni, in ultima istanza è uno solo, o invece utilizziamo una medesima parola per indicare realtà totalmente diverse?

«Eros» e «agape» – differenza e unità

3. All'amore tra uomo e donna, che non nasce dal pensare e dal volere ma in certo qual modo s'impone all'essere umano, l'antica Grecia ha dato il nome di *eros*. Diciamo già in anticipo che l'Antico Testamento greco usa solo due volte la parola *eros*, mentre il Nuovo Testamento non la usa mai: delle tre parole greche relative all'amore — *eros*, *philia* (amore di amicizia) e *agape* — gli scritti neotestamentari privilegiano l'ultima, che nel linguaggio greco era piuttosto messa ai margini. Quanto all'amore di amicizia (*philia*), esso viene ripreso e approfondito nel *Vangelo di Giovanni* per esprimere il rapporto tra Gesù e i suoi discepoli. La messa in disparte della parola *eros*, insieme alla nuova visione dell'amore che si esprime attraverso la parola *agape*, denota indubbiamente nella novità del cristianesimo qualcosa di essenziale, proprio a riguardo della comprensione dell'amore. Nella critica al cristianesimo che si è sviluppata con crescente radicalità a partire dall'illuminismo, questa novità è stata valutata in modo assolutamente negativo. Il cristianesimo, secondo Friedrich Nietzsche, avrebbe dato da bere del veleno all'*eros*, che, pur non morendone, ne avrebbe tratto la spinta a degenerare in vizio.[1] Con ciò il filosofo tedesco esprimeva una percezione molto diffusa: la Chiesa con i suoi comandamenti e divieti non ci rende forse amara la cosa più bella della vita? Non innalza forse cartelli di divieto proprio là dove la gioia, predisposta per noi dal Creatore, ci offre una felicità che ci fa pregustare qualcosa del Divino?

---

[1] Cfr *Jenseits von Gut und Böse*, IV, 168.

4. Ma è veramente così? Il cristianesimo ha davvero distrutto l'*eros*? Guardiamo al mondo pre-cristiano. I greci — senz'altro in analogia con altre culture — hanno visto nell'*eros* innanzitutto l'ebbrezza, la sopraffazione della ragione da parte di una «pazzia divina» che strappa l'uomo alla limitatezza della sua esistenza e, in questo essere sconvolto da una potenza divina, gli fa sperimentare la più alta beatitudine. Tutte le altre potenze tra il cielo e la terra appaiono, così, d'importanza secondaria: «*Omnia vincit amor*», afferma Virgilio nelle *Bucoliche* — l'amore vince tutto — e aggiunge: «*et nos cedamus amori*» — cediamo anche noi all'amore.[2] Nelle religioni questo atteggiamento si è tradotto nei culti della fertilità, ai quali appartiene la prostituzione «sacra» che fioriva in molti templi. L'*eros* venne quindi celebrato come forza divina, come comunione col Divino.

A questa forma di religione, che contrasta come potentissima tentazione con la fede nell'unico Dio, l'Antico Testamento si è opposto con massima fermezza, combattendola come perversione della religiosità. Con ciò però non ha per

[2] X, 69.

nulla rifiutato l'*eros* come tale, ma ha dichiarato guerra al suo stravolgimento distruttore, poiché la falsa divinizzazione dell'*eros*, che qui avviene, lo priva della sua dignità, lo disumanizza. Infatti, nel tempio, le prostitute, che devono donare l'ebbrezza del Divino, non vengono trattate come esseri umani e persone, ma servono soltanto come strumenti per suscitare la «pazzia divina»: in realtà, esse non sono dee, ma persone umane di cui si abusa. Per questo l'*eros* ebbro ed indisciplinato non è ascesa, «estasi» verso il Divino, ma caduta, degradazione dell'uomo. Così diventa evidente che l'*eros* ha bisogno di disciplina, di purificazione per donare all'uomo non il piacere di un istante, ma un certo pregustamento del vertice dell'esistenza, di quella beatitudine a cui tutto il nostro essere tende.

5. Due cose emergono chiaramente da questo rapido sguardo alla concezione dell'*eros* nella storia e nel presente. Innanzitutto che tra l'amore e il Divino esiste una qualche relazione: l'amore promette infinità, eternità — una realtà più grande e totalmente altra rispetto alla quotidianità del nostro esistere. Ma al contempo è apparso che la via per tale traguardo non sta semplicemente nel lasciarsi sopraffare dall'istinto. Sono necessarie purificazioni e maturazioni, che passano anche attraverso la strada della rinuncia. Questo non è rifiuto dell'*eros*, non è il suo «avvelenamento», ma la sua guarigione in vista della sua vera grandezza.

Ciò dipende innanzitutto dalla costituzione dell'essere umano, che è composto di corpo e di anima. L'uomo diventa veramente se stesso, quando corpo e anima si ritrovano in intima unità; la sfida dell'*eros* può dirsi veramente superata, quando questa unificazione è riuscita. Se l'uomo ambisce di essere solamente spirito e vuol rifiutare la carne come una eredità soltanto animalesca, allora spirito e corpo perdono la loro dignità. E se, d'altra parte, egli rinnega lo spirito e quindi considera la materia, il corpo, come realtà esclusiva, perde ugualmente la sua grandezza. L'epicureo Gassendi, scherzando, si rivolgeva a Cartesio col saluto: «O Anima!». E Cartesio replicava dicendo: «O Carne!».[3] Ma non sono né lo spirito né il corpo da soli ad amare: è l'uomo, la persona,

---

[3] Cfr R. DESCARTES, *Œuvres*, a cura di V. Cousin, vol. 12, Parigi 1824, p. 95 ss.

che ama come creatura unitaria, di cui fanno parte corpo e anima. Solo quando ambedue si fondono veramente in unità, l'uomo diventa pienamente se stesso. Solo in questo modo l'amore — l'*eros* — può maturare fino alla sua vera grandezza.

Oggi non di rado si rimprovera al cristianesimo del passato di esser stato avversario della corporeità; di fatto, tendenze in questo senso ci sono sempre state. Ma il modo di esaltare il corpo, a cui noi oggi assistiamo, è ingannevole. L'*eros* degradato a puro «sesso» diventa merce, una semplice «cosa» che si può comprare e vendere, anzi, l'uomo stesso diventa merce. In realtà, questo non è proprio il grande sì dell'uomo al suo corpo. Al contrario, egli ora considera il corpo e la sessualità come la parte soltanto materiale di sé da adoperare e sfruttare con calcolo. Una parte, peraltro, che egli non vede come un ambito della sua libertà, bensì come un qualcosa che, a modo suo, tenta di rendere insieme piacevole ed innocuo. In realtà, ci troviamo di fronte ad una degradazione del corpo umano, che non è più integrato nel tutto della libertà della nostra esistenza, non è più espressione viva della totalità del nostro essere, ma viene come respinto nel campo puramente biologico. L'apparente esaltazione del corpo può ben presto convertirsi in odio verso la corporeità. La fede cristiana, al contrario, ha considerato l'uomo sempre come essere uni-duale, nel quale spirito e materia si compenetrano a vicenda sperimentando proprio così ambedue una nuova nobiltà. Sì, l'*eros* vuole sollevarci « in estasi » verso il Divino, condurci al di là di noi stessi, ma proprio per questo richiede un cammino di ascesa, di rinunce, di purificazioni e di guarigioni.

6. Come dobbiamo configurarci concretamente questo cammino di ascesa e di purificazione? Come deve essere vissuto l'amore, perché si realizzi pienamente la sua promessa umana e divina? Una prima indicazione importante la possiamo trovare nel *Cantico dei Cantici*, uno dei libri dell'Antico Testamento ben noto ai mistici. Secondo l'interpretazione oggi prevalente, le poesie contenute in questo libro sono originariamente canti d'amore, forse previsti per una festa di nozze israelitica, nella quale dovevano esaltare l'amore coniugale. In tale contesto è molto istruttivo il fatto che, nel corso del libro, si trovano due parole diverse per indicare l'«amore». Dapprima vi è la parola «*dodim*» — un plurale che esprime l'amore ancora insicuro, in una situazione di ricerca indeterminata. Questa parola viene poi sostituita dalla parola «*ahabà*», che nella traduzione greca dell'Antico Testamento è resa col termine di simile suono «*agape*» che, come abbiamo visto, diventò l'espressione caratteristica per la concezione biblica dell'amore. In opposizione all'amore indeterminato e ancora in ricerca, questo vocabolo esprime l'esperienza dell'amore che diventa ora veramente scoperta dell'altro, superando il carattere egoistico prima chiaramente dominante. Adesso l'amore diventa cura dell'altro e per l'altro. Non cerca più se stesso, l'immersione nell'ebbrezza della felicità; cerca invece il bene dell'amato: diventa rinuncia, è pronto al sacrificio, anzi lo cerca.

Fa parte degli sviluppi dell'amore verso livelli più alti, verso le sue intime purificazioni, che esso cerchi ora la definitività, e ciò in un duplice senso: nel senso dell'esclusività — «solo quest'unica persona» — e nel senso del «per sempre». L'amore comprende la totalità dell'esistenza in ogni sua dimensione, anche in quella del tempo. Non potrebbe essere diversamente, perché la sua promessa mira al definitivo: l'amore mira all'eternità. Sì, amore è « estasi », ma estasi non nel senso di un momento di ebbrezza, ma estasi come cammino, come esodo permanente dall'io chiuso in se stesso verso la sua liberazione nel dono di sé, e proprio così verso il ritrovamento di sé, anzi verso la scoperta di Dio: « Chi cercherà di salvare la propria vita la perderà, chi invece la perde la salverà » (*Lc* 17, 33), dice Gesù — una sua affermazione che si ritrova nei Vangeli in diverse varianti (cfr *Mt* 10, 39; 16, 25; *Mc* 8, 35; *Lc* 9, 24; *Gv* 12, 25). Gesù con ciò descrive il suo personale cammino, che attraverso la croce lo conduce alla resurrezione: il cammino del chicco di grano che cade nella terra e muore e così porta molto frutto. Partendo dal centro del suo sacrificio personale e dell'amore che in esso giunge al suo compimento, egli con queste parole descrive anche l'essenza dell'amore e dell'esistenza umana in genere.

7. Le nostre riflessioni, inizialmente piuttosto filosofiche, sull'essenza dell'amore ci hanno ora condotto per interiore dinamica fino alla fede biblica. All'inizio si è posta la questione se i diversi, anzi opposti, significati della parola amore sottintendessero una qualche unità profonda o se invece dovessero restare slegati, l'uno accanto all'altro. Soprattutto, però, è emersa la questione se il messaggio sull'amore, a noi annunciato dalla Bibbia e dalla Tradizione della Chiesa, avesse qualcosa a che fare con la comune esperienza umana dell'amore o non si opponesse piuttosto ad essa. A tal proposito, ci siamo imbattuti nelle due parole fondamentali: *eros* come termine per significare l'amore «mondano» e *agape* come espressione per l'amore fondato sulla fede e da essa plasmato. Le due concezioni vengono spesso contrapposte come amore «ascendente» e amore «discendente». Vi sono altre classificazioni affini, come per esempio la distinzione tra amore possessivo e amore oblativo (*amor concupiscentiae – amor benevolentiae*), alla quale a volte viene aggiunto anche l'amore che mira al proprio tornaconto.

Nel dibattito filosofico e teologico queste distinzioni spesso sono state radicalizzate fino al punto di porle tra loro in contrapposizione: tipicamente cristiano sarebbe l'amore discendente, oblativo, l'*agape* appunto; la cultura non cristiana, invece, soprattutto quella greca, sarebbe caratterizzata dall'amore ascendente, bramoso e possessivo, cioè dall'*eros*. Se si volesse portare all'estremo questa antitesi, l'essenza del cristianesimo risulterebbe disarticolata dalle fondamentali relazioni vitali dell'esistere umano e costituirebbe un mondo a sé, da ritenere forse ammirevole, ma decisamente tagliato fuori dal complesso dell'esistenza umana. In realtà *eros* e *agape* — amore ascendente e amore discendente — non si lasciano mai separare completamente l'uno dall'altro. Quanto più ambedue, pur in dimensioni diverse, trovano la giusta unità nell'unica realtà dell'amore, tanto più si realizza la vera natura dell'amore in genere. Anche se l'*eros* inizialmente è soprattutto bramoso, ascendente — fascinazione per la grande promessa di felicità — nell'avvicinarsi poi all'altro si porrà sempre meno domande su di sé, cercherà sempre di più la felicità dell'altro, si preoccuperà sempre di più di lui, si donerà e desidererà «esserci per» l'altro. Così il momento dell'*agape* si inserisce in esso; altrimenti l'*eros* decade e perde anche la sua stessa natura. D'altra parte, l'uomo non può neanche vivere esclusivamente nell'amore oblativo, discendente. Non può sempre soltanto donare, deve anche ricevere. Chi vuol donare amore, deve egli stesso riceverlo in dono. Certo, l'uomo può — come ci dice il Signore — diventare sorgente dalla quale sgorgano fiumi di acqua viva (cfr *Gv* 7, 37-38). Ma per divenire una tale sorgente, egli stesso deve bere, sempre di nuovo, a quella prima, originaria sorgente che è Gesù Cristo, dal cui cuore trafitto scaturisce l'amore di Dio (cfr *Gv* 19, 34).

I Padri hanno visto simboleggiata in vari modi, nella narrazione della scala di Giacobbe, questa connessione inscindibile tra ascesa e discesa, tra l'*eros* che cerca Dio e l'*agape* che trasmette il dono ricevuto. In quel testo biblico si riferisce che il patriarca Giacobbe in sogno vide, sopra la pietra che gli serviva da guanciale, una scala che giungeva fino al cielo, sulla quale salivano e scendevano gli angeli di Dio (cfr *Gn* 28, 12; *Gv* 1, 51). Colpisce in modo particolare l'interpretazione che il Papa Gregorio Magno dà di questa visione nella sua *Regola pastorale*. Il pastore buono, egli dice, deve essere radicato nella contemplazione. Soltanto in questo modo, infatti, gli sarà possibile accogliere le necessità degli altri nel suo intimo, cosicché diventino sue: «*per pietatis viscera in se infirmitatem caeterorum transferat*».[4] San Gregorio, in questo contesto, fa riferimento a san Paolo che vien rapito in alto fin nei più grandi misteri di Dio e proprio così, quando ne discende, è in grado di farsi tutto a tutti (cfr 2 *Cor* 12, 2-4; 1 *Cor* 9, 22). Inoltre indica l'esempio di Mosè che sempre di nuovo entra nella tenda sacra restando in dialogo con Dio per poter così, a partire da Dio, essere a disposizione del suo popolo. «Dentro [la tenda] rapito in alto mediante la contemplazione, si lascia fuori [della tenda] incalzare dal peso dei sofferenti: *intus in contemplationem rapitur, foris infirmantium negotiis urgetur*».[5]

8. Abbiamo così trovato una prima risposta, ancora piuttosto generica, alle due domande suesposte: in fondo l'«amore» è un'unica realtà, seppur con diverse dimensioni; di volta in volta, l'una o l'altra dimensione può emergere maggiormente. Dove però le due dimensioni si distaccano completamente l'una dall'altra, si profila una ca-

[4] II, 5: *SCh* 381, 196.
[5] *Ibid.*, 198.

ricatura o in ogni caso una forma riduttiva dell'amore. E abbiamo anche visto sinteticamente che la fede biblica non costruisce un mondo parallelo o un mondo contrapposto rispetto a quell'originario fenomeno umano che è l'amore, ma accetta tutto l'uomo intervenendo nella sua ricerca di amore per purificarla, dischiudendogli al contempo nuove dimensioni. Questa novità della fede biblica si manifesta soprattutto in due punti, che meritano di essere sottolineati: l'immagine di Dio e l'immagine dell'uomo.

La novità della fede biblica

9. Vi è anzitutto la nuova immagine di Dio. Nelle culture che circondano il mondo della Bibbia, l'immagine di dio e degli dei rimane, alla fin fine, poco chiara e in sé contraddittoria. Nel cammino della fede biblica diventa invece sempre più chiaro ed univoco ciò che la preghiera fondamentale di Israele, lo *Sh^ema*, riassume nelle parole: «Ascolta, Israele: il Signore è il nostro Dio, il Signore è uno solo» (*Dt* 6, 4). Esiste un solo Dio, che è il Creatore del cielo e della terra e perciò è anche il Dio di tutti gli uomini. Due fatti in questa precisazione sono singolari: che veramente tutti gli altri dei non sono Dio e che tutta la realtà nella quale viviamo risale a Dio, è creata da Lui. Certamente, l'idea di una creazione esiste anche altrove, ma solo qui risulta assolutamente chiaro che non un dio qualsiasi, ma l'unico vero Dio, Egli stesso, è l'autore dell'intera realtà; essa proviene dalla potenza della sua Parola creatrice. Ciò significa che questa sua creatura gli è cara, perché appunto da Lui stesso è stata voluta, da Lui «fatta». E così appare ora il secondo elemento importante: questo Dio ama l'uomo. La potenza divina che Aristotele, al culmine della filosofia greca, cercò di cogliere mediante la riflessione, è sì per ogni essere oggetto del desiderio e dell'amore — come realtà amata questa divinità muove il mondo[6] —, ma essa stessa non ha bisogno di niente e non ama, soltanto viene amata. L'unico Dio in cui Israele crede, invece, ama personalmente. Il suo amore, inoltre, è un amore elettivo: tra tutti i popoli Egli sceglie Israele e lo ama — con lo scopo però di guarire, proprio in tal modo, l'intera umanità. Egli ama,

[6] Cfr *Metafisica*, XII, 7.

e questo suo amore può essere qualificato senz'altro come *eros*, che tuttavia è anche e totalmente *agape*.[7]

Soprattutto i profeti Osea ed Ezechiele hanno descritto questa passione di Dio per il suo popolo con ardite immagini erotiche. Il rapporto di Dio con Israele viene illustrato mediante le metafore del fidanzamento e del matrimonio; di conseguenza, l'idolatria è adulterio e prostituzione. Con ciò si accenna concretamente — come abbiamo visto — ai culti della fertilità con il loro abuso dell'*eros*, ma al contempo viene anche descritto il rapporto di fedeltà tra Israele e il suo Dio. La storia d'amore di Dio con Israele consiste, in profondità, nel fatto che Egli dona la *Torah*, apre cioè gli occhi a Israele sulla vera natura dell'uomo e gli indica la strada del vero umanesimo. Tale storia consiste nel fatto che l'uomo, vivendo nella fedeltà all'unico Dio, sperimenta se stesso come colui che è amato da Dio e scopre la gioia nella verità, nella giustizia — la gioia in Dio che diventa la sua essenziale felicità: «Chi altri

---

[7] Cfr Pseudo Dionigi Areopagita che, nel suo *Sui nomi divini*, IV, 12-14: *PG* 3, 709-713, chiama Dio nello stesso tempo *eros* e *agape*.

avrò per me in cielo? Fuori di te nulla bramo sulla terra ... Il mio bene è stare vicino a Dio» (*Sal* 73 [72], 25. 28).

10. L'*eros* di Dio per l'uomo — come abbiamo detto — è insieme totalmente *agape*. Non soltanto perché viene donato del tutto gratuitamente, senza alcun merito precedente, ma anche perché è amore che perdona. Soprattutto Osea ci mostra la dimensione dell'*agape* nell'amore di Dio per l'uomo, che supera di gran lunga l'aspetto della gratuità. Israele ha commesso «adulterio», ha rotto l'Alleanza; Dio dovrebbe giudicarlo e ripudiarlo. Proprio qui si rivela però che Dio è Dio e non uomo: «Come potrei abbandonarti, Efraim, come consegnarti ad altri, Israele? ... Il mio cuore si commuove dentro di me, il mio intimo freme di compassione. Non darò sfogo all'ardore della mia ira, non tornerò a distruggere Efraim, perché sono Dio e non uomo; sono il Santo in mezzo a te» (*Os* 11, 8-9). L'amore appassionato di Dio per il suo popolo — per l'uomo — è nello stesso tempo un amore che perdona. Esso è talmente grande da rivolgere Dio contro se stesso, il suo amore contro la sua giustizia. Il cristiano vede, in questo, già profilarsi velatamente il mistero della Croce: Dio ama tanto l'uomo che, facendosi uomo Egli stesso, lo segue fin nella morte e in questo modo riconcilia giustizia e amore.

L'aspetto filosofico e storico-religioso da rilevare in questa visione della Bibbia sta nel fatto che, da una parte, ci troviamo di fronte ad un'immagine strettamente metafisica di Dio: Dio è in assoluto la sorgente originaria di ogni essere; ma questo principio creativo di tutte le cose — il *Logos*, la ragione primordiale — è al contempo un amante con tutta la passione di un vero amore. In questo modo l'*eros* è nobilitato al massimo, ma contemporaneamente così purificato da fondersi con l'*agape*. Da ciò possiamo comprendere che la ricezione del *Cantico dei Cantici* nel canone della Sacra Scrittura sia stata spiegata ben presto nel senso che quei canti d'amore descrivono, in fondo, il rapporto di Dio con l'uomo e dell'uomo con Dio. In questo modo il *Cantico dei Cantici* è diventato, nella letteratura cristiana come in quella giudaica, una sorgente di conoscenza e di esperienza mistica, in cui si esprime l'essenza della fede biblica: sì, esiste una unificazione dell'uomo con Dio — il sogno originario dell'uomo —, ma questa unificazione non è un fondersi insieme, un affondare nell'oceano anonimo del Divino; è unità che crea amore, in cui entrambi — Dio e l'uomo — restano se stessi e tuttavia diventano pienamente una cosa sola: «Chi si unisce al Signore forma con lui un solo spirito», dice san Paolo (*1 Cor* 6, 17).

11. La prima novità della fede biblica consiste, come abbiamo visto, nell'immagine di Dio; la seconda, con essa essenzialmente connessa, la troviamo nell'immagine dell'uomo. Il racconto biblico della creazione parla della solitudine del primo uomo, Adamo, al quale Dio vuole affiancare un aiuto. Fra tutte le creature, nessuna può essere per l'uomo quell'aiuto di cui ha bisogno, sebbene a tutte le bestie selvatiche e a tutti gli uccelli egli abbia dato un nome, integrandoli così nel contesto della sua vita. Allora, da una costola dell'uomo, Dio plasma la donna. Ora Adamo trova l'aiuto di cui ha bisogno: «Questa volta essa è carne dalla mia carne e osso dalle mie ossa» (*Gn* 2, 23). È possibile vedere sullo sfondo di questo racconto concezioni quali appaiono, per esempio, anche nel mito riferito da Platone, secondo cui l'uomo originariamente era sferico, perché completo in se stesso ed autosufficiente. Ma, come punizione per la sua superbia, venne da Zeus dimezzato, così che ora sempre anela all'altra sua metà ed è in cammino verso di essa per ritrovare la sua interezza.[8] Nel racconto biblico non si parla di punizione; l'idea però che l'uomo sia in qualche modo incompleto, costituzionalmente in cammino per trovare nell'altro la parte integrante per la sua interezza, l'idea cioè che egli solo nella comunione con l'altro sesso possa diventare «completo», è senz'altro presente. E così il racconto biblico si conclude con una profezia su Adamo: «Per questo l'uomo abbandonerà suo padre e sua madre e si unirà a sua moglie e i due saranno una sola carne» (*Gn* 2, 24).

Due sono qui gli aspetti importanti: l'*eros* è come radicato nella natura stessa dell'uomo; Adamo è in ricerca e «abbandona suo padre e sua madre» per trovare la donna; solo nel loro insieme rappresentano l'interezza dell'umanità, diventano «una sola carne». Non meno importante è il

[8] Cfr *Il Convito*, XIV-XV, 189c-192d.

secondo aspetto: in un orientamento fondato nella creazione, l'*eros* rimanda l'uomo al matrimonio, a un legame caratterizzato da unicità e definitività; così, e solo così, si realizza la sua intima destinazione. All'immagine del Dio monoteistico corrisponde il matrimonio monogamico. Il matrimonio basato su un amore esclusivo e definitivo diventa l'icona del rapporto di Dio con il suo popolo e viceversa: il modo di amare di Dio diventa la misura dell'amore umano. Questo stretto nesso tra *eros* e matrimonio nella Bibbia quasi non trova paralleli nella letteratura al di fuori di essa.

Gesù Cristo – l'amore incarnato di Dio

12. Anche se finora abbiamo parlato prevalentemente dell'Antico Testamento, tuttavia l'intima compenetrazione dei due Testamenti come unica Scrittura della fede cristiana si è già resa visibile. La vera novità del Nuovo Testamento non sta in nuove idee, ma nella figura stessa di Cristo, che dà carne e sangue ai concetti — un realismo inaudito. Già nell'Antico Testamento la novità biblica non consiste semplicemente in nozioni astratte, ma nell'agire imprevedibile e in certo senso inaudito di Dio. Questo agire di Dio acquista ora la sua forma drammatica nel fatto che, in Gesù Cristo, Dio stesso insegue la «pecorella smarrita», l'umanità sofferente e perduta. Quando Gesù nelle sue parabole parla del pastore che va dietro alla pecorella smarrita, della donna che cerca la dracma, del padre che va incontro al figliol prodigo e lo abbraccia, queste non sono soltanto parole, ma costituiscono la spiegazione del suo stesso essere ed operare. Nella sua morte in croce si compie quel volgersi di Dio contro se stesso nel quale Egli si dona per rialzare l'uomo e salvarlo — amore, questo, nella sua forma più radicale. Lo sguardo rivolto al fianco squarciato di Cristo, di cui parla Giovanni (cfr 19, 37), comprende ciò che è stato il punto di partenza di questa Lettera enciclica: «Dio è amore» (*1 Gv* 4, 8). È lì che questa verità può essere contemplata. E partendo da lì deve ora definirsi che cosa sia l'amore. A partire da questo sguardo il cristiano trova la strada del suo vivere e del suo amare.

13. A questo atto di offerta Gesù ha dato una presenza duratura attraverso l'istituzione dell'Eucaristia, durante l'Ultima Cena. Egli anticipa la sua morte e resurrezione donando già in quell'ora ai suoi discepoli nel pane e nel vino se stesso, il suo corpo e il suo sangue come nuova manna (cfr *Gv* 6, 31-33). Se il mondo antico aveva sognato che, in fondo, vero cibo dell'uomo — ciò di cui egli come uomo vive — fosse il *Logos*, la sapienza eterna, adesso questo *Logos* è diventato veramente per noi nutrimento — come amore. L'Eucaristia ci attira nell'atto oblativo di Gesù. Noi non riceviamo soltanto in modo statico il *Logos* incarnato, ma veniamo coinvolti nella dinamica della sua donazione. L'immagine del matrimonio tra Dio e Israele diventa realtà in un modo prima inconcepibile: ciò che era lo stare di fronte a Dio diventa ora, attraverso la partecipazione alla donazione di Gesù, partecipazione al suo corpo e al suo sangue, diventa unione. La «mistica» del Sacramento che si fonda nell'abbassamento di Dio verso di noi è di ben altra portata e conduce ben più in alto di quanto qualsiasi mistico innalzamento dell'uomo potrebbe realizzare.

14. Ora però c'è da far attenzione ad un altro aspetto: la «mistica» del Sacramento ha un carattere sociale, perché nella comunione sacramentale io vengo unito al Signore come tutti gli altri comunicanti: «Poiché c'è un solo pane, noi, pur essendo molti, siamo un corpo solo: tutti infatti partecipiamo dell'unico pane», dice san Paolo (*1 Cor* 10, 17). L'unione con Cristo è allo stesso tempo unione con tutti gli altri ai quali Egli si dona. Io non posso avere Cristo solo per me; posso appartenergli soltanto in unione con tutti quelli che sono diventati o diventeranno suoi. La comunione mi tira fuori di me stesso verso di Lui, e così anche verso l'unità con tutti i cristiani. Diventiamo «un solo corpo», fusi insieme in un'unica esistenza. Amore per Dio e amore per il prossimo sono ora veramente uniti: il Dio incarnato ci attrae tutti a sé. Da ciò si comprende come *agape* sia ora diventata anche un nome dell'Eucaristia: in essa l'*agape* di Dio viene a noi corporalmente per continuare il suo operare in noi e attraverso di noi. Solo a partire da questo fondamento cristologico-sacramentale si può capire correttamente l'insegnamento di Gesù sull'amore. Il passaggio che Egli fa fare dalla

Legge e dai Profeti al duplice comandamento dell'amore verso Dio e verso il prossimo, la derivazione di tutta l'esistenza di fede dalla centralità di questo precetto, non è semplice morale che poi possa sussistere autonomamente accanto alla fede in Cristo e alla sua riattualizzazione nel Sacramento: fede, culto ed *ethos* si compenetrano a vicenda come un'unica realtà che si configura nell'incontro con l'*agape* di Dio. La consueta contrapposizione di culto ed etica qui semplicemente cade. Nel «culto» stesso, nella comunione eucaristica è contenuto l'essere amati e l'amare a propria volta gli altri. Un'Eucaristia che non si traduca in amore concretamente praticato è in se stessa frammentata. Reciprocamente — come dovremo ancora considerare in modo più dettagliato — il «comandamento» dell'amore diventa possibile solo perché non è soltanto esigenza: l'amore può essere «comandato» perché prima è donato.

15. È a partire da questo principio che devono essere comprese anche le grandi parabole di Gesù. Il ricco epulone (cfr *Lc* 16, 19-31) implora dal luogo della dannazione che i suoi fratelli vengano informati su ciò che succede a colui che ha disinvoltamente ignorato il povero in necessità. Gesù raccoglie per così dire tale grido di aiuto e se ne fa eco per metterci in guardia, per riportarci sulla retta via. La parabola del buon Samaritano (cfr *Lc* 10, 25-37) conduce soprattutto a due importanti chiarificazioni. Mentre il concetto di «prossimo» era riferito, fino ad allora, essenzialmente ai connazionali e agli stranieri che si erano stanziati nella terra d'Israele e quindi alla comunità solidale di un paese e di un popolo, adesso questo limite viene abolito. Chiunque ha bisogno di me e io posso aiutarlo, è il mio prossimo. Il concetto di prossimo viene universalizzato e rimane tuttavia concreto. Nonostante la sua estensione a tutti gli uomini, non si riduce all'espressione di un amore generico ed astratto, in se stesso poco impegnativo, ma richiede il mio impegno pratico qui ed ora. Rimane compito della Chiesa interpretare sempre di nuovo questo collegamento tra lontananza e vicinanza in vista della vita pratica dei suoi membri. Infine, occorre qui rammentare, in modo particolare, la grande parabola del Giudizio finale (cfr *Mt* 25, 31-46), in cui l'amore diviene il criterio per la decisione definitiva sul valore o il disvalore di una vita umana. Gesù si identifica con i bisognosi: affamati, assetati, forestieri, nudi, malati, carcerati. «Ogni volta che avete fatto queste cose a uno solo di questi miei fratelli più piccoli, l'avete fatto a me» (*Mt* 25, 40). Amore di Dio e amore del prossimo si fondono insieme: nel più piccolo incontriamo Gesù stesso e in Gesù incontriamo Dio.

Amore di Dio e amore del prossimo

16. Dopo aver riflettuto sull'essenza dell'amore e sul suo significato nella fede biblica, rimane una duplice domanda circa il nostro atteggiamento: è veramente possibile amare Dio pur non vedendolo? E: l'amore si può comandare? Contro il duplice comandamento dell'amore esiste la duplice obiezione, che risuona in queste domande. Nessuno ha mai visto Dio — come potremmo amarlo? E inoltre: l'amore non si può comandare; è in definitiva un sentimento che può esserci o non esserci, ma che non può essere creato dalla volontà. La Scrittura sembra avallare la prima obiezione quando afferma: «Se uno dicesse: "Io amo Dio" e odiasse il suo fratello, è un mentitore. Chi infatti non ama il proprio fratello che vede, non può amare Dio che non vede» (*1 Gv* 4, 20). Ma questo testo non esclude affatto l'amore di Dio come qualcosa di impossibile; al contrario, nell'intero contesto della *Prima Lettera di Giovanni* ora citata, tale amore viene richiesto esplicitamente. Viene sottolineato il collegamento inscindibile tra amore di Dio e amore del prossimo. Entrambi si richiamano così strettamente che l'affermazione dell'amore di Dio diventa una menzogna, se l'uomo si chiude al prossimo o addirittura lo odia. Il versetto giovanneo si deve interpretare piuttosto nel senso che l'amore per il prossimo è una strada per incontrare anche Dio e che il chiudere gli occhi di fronte al prossimo rende ciechi anche di fronte a Dio.

17.   In effetti, nessuno ha mai visto Dio così come Egli è in se stesso. E tuttavia Dio non è per noi totalmente invisibile, non è rimasto per noi semplicemente inaccessibile. Dio ci ha amati per primo, dice la *Lettera di Giovanni* citata (cfr 4, 10) e questo amore di Dio è apparso in mezzo a noi, si è fatto visibile in quanto Egli «ha mandato il suo

Figlio unigenito nel mondo, perché noi avessimo la vita per lui» (*1 Gv* 4, 9). Dio si è fatto visibile: in Gesù noi possiamo vedere il Padre (cfr *Gv* 14, 9). Di fatto esiste una molteplice visibilità di Dio. Nella storia d'amore che la Bibbia ci racconta, Egli ci viene incontro, cerca di conquistarci — fino all'Ultima Cena, fino al Cuore trafitto sulla croce, fino alle apparizioni del Risorto e alle grandi opere mediante le quali Egli, attraverso l'azione degli Apostoli, ha guidato il cammino della Chiesa nascente. Anche nella successiva storia della Chiesa il Signore non è rimasto assente: sempre di nuovo ci viene incontro — attraverso uomini nei quali Egli traspare; attraverso la sua Parola, nei Sacramenti, specialmente nell'Eucaristia. Nella liturgia della Chiesa, nella sua preghiera, nella comunità viva dei credenti, noi sperimentiamo l'amore di Dio, percepiamo la sua presenza e impariamo in questo modo anche a riconoscerla nel nostro quotidiano. Egli per primo ci ha amati e continua ad amarci per primo; per questo anche noi possiamo rispondere con l'amore. Dio non ci ordina un sentimento che non possiamo suscitare in noi stessi. Egli ci ama, ci fa vedere e sperimentare il suo amore e, da questo «prima» di Dio, può come risposta spuntare l'amore anche in noi.

Nello sviluppo di questo incontro si rivela con chiarezza che l'amore non è soltanto un sentimento. I sentimenti vanno e vengono. Il sentimento può essere una meravigliosa scintilla iniziale, ma non è la totalità dell'amore. Abbiamo all'inizio parlato del processo delle purificazioni e delle maturazioni, attraverso le quali l'*eros* diventa pienamente se stesso, diventa amore nel pieno significato della parola. È proprio della maturità dell'amore coinvolgere tutte le potenzialità dell'uomo ed includere, per così dire, l'uomo nella sua interezza. L'incontro con le manifestazioni visibili dell'amore di Dio può suscitare in noi il sentimento della gioia, che nasce dall'esperienza dell'essere amati. Ma tale incontro chiama in causa anche la nostra volontà e il nostro intelletto. Il riconoscimento del Dio vivente è una via verso l'amore, e il sì della nostra volontà alla sua unisce intelletto, volontà e sentimento nell'atto totalizzante dell'amore. Questo però è un processo che rimane continuamente in cammino: l'amore non è mai «concluso» e completato; si trasforma nel corso della vita, matura e proprio per questo rimane fedele a se stesso. *Idem velle atque idem nolle* [9] — volere la stessa cosa e rifiutare la stessa cosa, è quanto gli antichi hanno riconosciuto come autentico contenuto dell'amore: il diventare l'uno simile all'altro, che conduce alla comunanza del volere e del pensare. La storia d'amore tra Dio e l'uomo consiste appunto nel fatto che questa comunione di volontà cresce in comunione di pensiero e di sentimento e, così, il nostro volere e la volontà di Dio coincidono sempre di più: la volontà di Dio non è più per me una volontà estranea, che i comandamenti mi impongono dall'esterno, ma è la mia stessa volontà, in base all'esperienza che, di fatto, Dio è più intimo a me di quanto lo sia io stesso.[10] Allora cresce l'abbandono in Dio e Dio diventa la nostra gioia (cfr *Sal* 73 [72], 23-28).

18. Si rivela così possibile l'amore del prossimo nel senso enunciato dalla Bibbia, da Gesù. Esso consiste appunto nel fatto che io amo, in Dio e con Dio, anche la persona che non gradisco o neanche conosco. Questo può realizzarsi solo a partire dall'intimo incontro con Dio, un incontro che è diventato comunione di volontà

---

[9] Sallustio, *De coniuratione Catilinae*, XX, 4.
[10] Cfr sant'Agostino, *Confessiones*, III, 6, 11: *CCL* 27, 32.

arrivando fino a toccare il sentimento. Allora imparo a guardare quest'altra persona non più soltanto con i miei occhi e con i miei sentimenti, ma secondo la prospettiva di Gesù Cristo. Il suo amico è mio amico. Al di là dell'apparenza esteriore dell'altro scorgo la sua interiore attesa di un gesto di amore, di attenzione, che io non faccio arrivare a lui soltanto attraverso le organizzazioni a ciò deputate, accettandolo magari come necessità politica. Io vedo con gli occhi di Cristo e posso dare all'altro ben più che le cose esternamente necessarie: posso donargli lo sguardo di amore di cui egli ha bisogno. Qui si mostra l'interazione necessaria tra amore di Dio e amore del prossimo, di cui la *Prima Lettera di Giovanni* parla con tanta insistenza. Se il contatto con Dio manca del tutto nella mia vita, posso vedere nell'altro sempre soltanto l'altro e non riesco a riconoscere in lui l'immagine divina. Se però nella mia vita tralascio completamente l'attenzione per l'altro, volendo essere solamente «pio» e compiere i miei «doveri religiosi», allora s'inaridisce anche il rapporto con Dio. Allora questo rapporto è soltanto «corretto», ma senza amore. Solo la mia disponibilità ad andare incontro al prossimo, a mostrargli amore, mi rende sensibile anche di fronte a Dio. Solo il servizio al prossimo apre i miei occhi su quello che Dio fa per me e su come Egli mi ama. I santi — pensiamo ad esempio alla beata Teresa di Calcutta — hanno attinto la loro capacità di amare il prossimo, in modo sempre nuovo, dal loro incontro col Signore eucaristico e, reciprocamente questo incontro ha acquisito il suo realismo e la sua profondità proprio nel loro servizio agli altri. Amore di Dio e amore del prossimo sono inseparabili, sono un unico comandamento. Entrambi però vivono dell'amore preveniente di Dio che ci ha amati per primo. Così non si tratta più di un «comandamento» dall'esterno che ci impone l'impossibile, bensì di un'esperienza dell'amore donata dall'interno, un amore che, per sua natura, deve essere ulteriormente partecipato ad altri. L'amore cresce attraverso l'amore. L'amore è «divino» perché viene da Dio e ci unisce a Dio e, mediante questo processo unificante, ci trasforma in un Noi che supera le nostre divisioni e ci fa diventare una cosa sola, fino a che, alla fine, Dio sia «tutto in tutti» (*1 Cor* 15, 28).

SECONDA PARTE

CARITAS – L'ESERCIZIO DELL'AMORE
DA PARTE DELLA CHIESA
QUALE «COMUNITÀ D'AMORE»

La carità della Chiesa come manifestazione dell'amore trinitario

19. «Se vedi la carità, vedi la Trinità» scriveva sant'Agostino.[11] Nelle riflessioni che precedono, abbiamo potuto fissare il nostro sguardo sul Trafitto (cfr *Gv* 19, 37; *Zc* 12, 10), riconoscendo il disegno del Padre che, mosso dall'amore (cfr *Gv* 3, 16), ha inviato il Figlio unigenito nel mondo per redimere l'uomo. Morendo sulla croce, Gesù — come riferisce l'evangelista — «emise lo spirito» (cfr *Gv* 19, 30), preludio di quel dono dello Spirito Santo che Egli avrebbe realizzato dopo la risurrezione (cfr *Gv* 20, 22). Si sarebbe attuata così la promessa dei «fiumi di acqua viva» che, grazie all'effusione dello Spirito, sarebbero sgorgati dal cuore dei credenti (cfr *Gv* 7, 38-39). Lo Spirito, infatti, è quella potenza interiore che armonizza il loro cuore col cuore di Cristo e li muove ad amare i fratelli come li ha amati Lui, quando si è curvato a lavare i piedi dei discepoli

[11] *De Trinitate,* VIII, 8, 12: *CCL* 50, 287.

(cfr *Gv* 13, 1-13) e soprattutto quando ha donato la sua vita per tutti (cfr *Gv* 13, 1; 15, 13).

Lo Spirito è anche forza che trasforma il cuore della Comunità ecclesiale, affinché sia nel mondo testimone dell'amore del Padre, che vuole fare dell'umanità, nel suo Figlio, un'unica famiglia. Tutta l'attività della Chiesa è espressione di un amore che cerca il bene integrale dell'uomo: cerca la sua evangelizzazione mediante la Parola e i Sacramenti, impresa tante volte eroica nelle sue realizzazioni storiche; e cerca la sua promozione nei vari ambiti della vita e dell'attività umana. Amore è pertanto il servizio che la Chiesa svolge per venire costantemente incontro alle sofferenze e ai bisogni, anche materiali, degli uomini. È su questo aspetto, su questo *servizio della carità*, che desidero soffermarmi in questa seconda parte dell'Enciclica.

La carità come compito della Chiesa

20. L'amore del prossimo radicato nell'amore di Dio è anzitutto un compito per ogni singolo fedele, ma è anche un compito per l'intera comunità ecclesiale, e questo a tutti i suoi livelli: dalla comunità locale alla Chiesa particolare fino alla Chiesa universale nella sua globalità. Anche la Chiesa in quanto comunità deve praticare l'amore. Conseguenza di ciò è che l'amore ha bisogno anche di organizzazione quale presupposto per un servizio comunitario ordinato. La coscienza di tale compito ha avuto rilevanza costitutiva nella Chiesa fin dai suoi inizi: «Tutti coloro che erano diventati credenti stavano insieme e tenevano ogni cosa in comune; chi aveva proprietà e sostanze le vendeva e ne faceva parte a tutti, secondo il bisogno di ciascuno» (*At* 2, 44-45). Luca ci racconta questo in connessione con una sorta di definizione della Chiesa, tra i cui elementi costitutivi egli annovera l'adesione all'«insegnamento degli Apostoli», alla «comunione» (*koinonia*), alla «frazione del pane» e alla «preghiera» (cfr *At* 2, 42). L'elemento della «comunione» (*koinonia*), qui inizialmente non specificato, viene concretizzato nei versetti sopra citati: essa consiste appunto nel fatto che i credenti hanno tutto in comune e che, in mezzo a loro, la differenza tra ricchi e poveri non sussiste più (cfr anche *At* 4, 32-37). Con il crescere della Chiesa, questa forma radicale di comunione materiale non ha potuto, per la verità, essere mantenuta. Il nucleo essenziale è però rimasto: all'interno della comunità dei credenti non deve esservi una forma di povertà tale che a qualcuno siano negati i beni necessari per una vita dignitosa.

21. Un passo decisivo nella difficile ricerca di soluzioni per realizzare questo fondamentale principio ecclesiale diventa visibile in quella scelta di sette uomini che fu l'inizio dell'ufficio diaconale (cfr *At* 6, 5-6). Nella Chiesa delle origini, infatti, si era creata, nella distribuzione quotidiana alle vedove, una disparità tra la parte di lingua ebraica e quella di lingua greca. Gli Apostoli, ai quali erano affidati innanzitutto la «preghiera» (Eucaristia e Liturgia) e il «servizio della Parola», si sentirono eccessivamente appesantiti dal «servizio delle mense»; decisero pertanto di riservare a sé il ministero principale e di creare per l'altro compito, pur necessario nella Chiesa, un consesso di sette persone. Anche questo gruppo però non doveva svolgere un servizio semplicemente tecnico di distribuzione: dovevano essere uomini «pieni di Spirito e di saggezza» (cfr *At* 6, 1-6). Ciò significa che il servizio sociale che dovevano effettuare era assolutamente concreto, ma al contempo era senz'altro anche un servizio spirituale; il loro perciò era un vero ufficio spirituale, che realizzava un compito essenziale della Chiesa, quello dell'amore ben ordinato del prossimo. Con la formazione di questo consesso dei Sette, la «diaconia» — il servizio dell'amore del prossimo esercitato comunitariamente e in modo ordinato — era ormai instaurata nella struttura fondamentale della Chiesa stessa.

22. Con il passare degli anni e con il progressivo diffondersi della Chiesa, l'esercizio della carità si confermò come uno dei suoi ambiti essenziali, insieme con l'amministrazione dei Sacramenti e l'annuncio della Parola: praticare l'amore verso le vedove e gli orfani, verso i carcerati, i malati e i bisognosi di ogni genere appartiene alla sua essenza tanto quanto il servizio dei Sacramenti e l'annuncio del Vangelo. La Chiesa non può trascurare il servizio della carità così come non può tralasciare i Sacramenti e la Parola. Bastino alcuni riferimenti per dimostrarlo. Il martire Giustino († ca. 155) descrive, nel contesto della celebrazione domenicale dei cristiani, anche la loro attività caritativa, collegata con l'Eucaristia come tale. Gli abbienti fanno la loro offerta nella misura delle loro possibilità, ognuno quanto vuole; il Vescovo se ne serve poi per sostenere gli orfani, le vedove e coloro che a causa di malattia o per altri motivi si trovano in necessità, come anche i carcerati e i forestieri.[12] Il grande scrittore cristiano Tertulliano († dopo il 220) racconta come la premura dei cristiani verso ogni genere di bisognosi suscitasse la meraviglia dei pagani.[13] E quando Ignazio di Antiochia († ca. 117) qualifica la Chiesa di Roma come colei che «presiede nella carità (*agape*)»,[14] si può ritenere che egli, con questa definizione, intendesse esprimerne in qualche modo anche la concreta attività caritativa.

23. In questo contesto può risultare utile un riferimento alle primitive strutture giuridiche riguardanti il servizio della carità nella Chiesa. Verso la metà del IV secolo prende forma in Egitto la cosiddetta «*diaconia*»; essa è nei singoli mona-

---

[12] Cfr *I Apologia*, 67: *PG* 6, 429.
[13] Cfr *Apologeticum* 39, 7: *PL* 1, 468.
[14] *Ep. ad Rom., Inscr. PG* 5, 801.

steri l'istituzione responsabile per il complesso delle attività assistenziali, per il servizio della carità appunto. Da questi inizi si sviluppa in Egitto fino al VI secolo una corporazione con piena capacità giuridica, a cui le autorità civili affidano addirittura una parte del grano per la distribuzione pubblica. In Egitto non solo ogni monastero ma anche ogni diocesi finisce per avere la sua *diaconia* — una istituzione che si sviluppa poi sia in oriente sia in occidente. Papa Gregorio Magno († 604) riferisce della *diaconia* di Napoli. Per Roma le diaconie sono documentate a partire dal VII e VIII secolo; ma naturalmente già prima, e fin dagli inizi, l'attività assistenziale per i poveri e i sofferenti, secondo i principi della vita cristiana esposti negli *Atti degli Apostoli*, era parte essenziale della Chiesa di Roma. Questo compito trova una sua vivace espressione nella figura del diacono Lorenzo († 258). La descrizione drammatica del suo martirio era nota già a sant'Ambrogio († 397) e ci mostra, nel suo nucleo, sicuramente l'autentica figura del Santo. A lui, quale responsabile della cura dei poveri di Roma, era stato concesso qualche tempo, dopo la cattura dei suoi confratelli e del Papa, per raccogliere i tesori della

Chiesa e consegnarli alle autorità civili. Lorenzo distribuì il denaro disponibile ai poveri e li presentò poi alle autorità come il vero tesoro della Chiesa.[15] Comunque si valuti l'attendibilità storica di tali particolari, Lorenzo è rimasto presente nella memoria della Chiesa come grande esponente della carità ecclesiale.

24. Un accenno alla figura dell'imperatore Giuliano l'Apostata († 363) può mostrare ancora una volta quanto essenziale fosse per la Chiesa dei primi secoli la carità organizzata e praticata. Bambino di sei anni, Giuliano aveva assistito all'assassinio di suo padre, di suo fratello e di altri familiari da parte delle guardie del palazzo imperiale; egli addebitò questa brutalità — a torto o a ragione — all'imperatore Costanzo, che si spacciava per un grande cristiano. Con ciò la fede cristiana risultò per lui screditata una volta per tutte. Divenuto imperatore, decise di restaurare il paganesimo, l'antica religione romana, ma al contempo di riformarlo, in modo che potesse diventare realmente la forza trainante dell'impero.

---

[15] Cfr SANT'AMBROGIO, *De officiis ministrorum*, II, 28, 140: *PL* 16, 141.

In questa prospettiva si ispirò ampiamente al cristianesimo. Instaurò una gerarchia di metropoliti e sacerdoti. I sacerdoti dovevano curare l'amore per Dio e per il prossimo. In una delle sue lettere[16] aveva scritto che l'unico aspetto del cristianesimo che lo colpiva era l'attività caritativa della Chiesa. Fu quindi un punto determinante, per il suo nuovo paganesimo, affiancare al sistema di carità della Chiesa un'attività equivalente della sua religione. I «Galilei» — così egli diceva — avevano conquistato in questo modo la loro popolarità. Li si doveva emulare ed anche superare. L'imperatore in questo modo confermava dunque che la carità era una caratteristica decisiva della comunità cristiana, della Chiesa.

25. Giunti a questo punto, raccogliamo dalle nostre riflessioni due dati essenziali:

a) L'intima natura della Chiesa si esprime in un triplice compito: annuncio della Parola di Dio (*kerygma-martyria*), celebrazione dei Sacramenti (*leiturgia*), servizio della carità (*diakonia*). Sono

---

[16] Cfr *Ep.* 83: J. BIDEZ, *L'Empereur Julien. Œuvres complètes*, Parigi 1960², t. I, 2ª, p. 145.

compiti che si presuppongono a vicenda e non possono essere separati l'uno dall'altro. La carità non è per la Chiesa una specie di attività di assistenza sociale che si potrebbe anche lasciare ad altri, ma appartiene alla sua natura, è espressione irrinunciabile della sua stessa essenza.[17]

b) La Chiesa è la famiglia di Dio nel mondo. In questa famiglia non deve esserci nessuno che soffra per mancanza del necessario. Al contempo però la *caritas-agape* travalica le frontiere della Chiesa; la parabola del buon Samaritano rimane come criterio di misura, impone l'universalità dell'amore che si volge verso il bisognoso incontrato «per caso» (cfr *Lc* 10, 31), chiunque egli sia. Ferma restando questa universalità del comandamento dell'amore, vi è però anche un'esigenza specificamente ecclesiale — quella appunto che nella Chiesa stessa, in quanto famiglia, nessun membro soffra perché nel bisogno. In questo senso vale la parola della *Lettera ai Galati*: «Poiché

---

[17] Cfr CONGREGAZIONE PER I VESCOVI, Direttorio per il ministero pastorale dei Vescovi *Apostolorum Successores* (22 febbraio 2004), 194: Città del Vaticano 2004, 2ª, 205-206.

dunque ne abbiamo l'occasione, operiamo il bene verso tutti, soprattutto verso i fratelli nella fede» (6, 10).

Giustizia e carità

26. Fin dall'Ottocento contro l'attività caritativa della Chiesa è stata sollevata un'obiezione, sviluppata poi con insistenza soprattutto dal pensiero marxista. I poveri, si dice, non avrebbero bisogno di opere di carità, bensì di giustizia. Le opere di carità — le elemosine — in realtà sarebbero, per i ricchi, un modo di sottrarsi all'instaurazione della giustizia e di acquietare la coscienza, conservando le proprie posizioni e frodando i poveri nei loro diritti. Invece di contribuire attraverso singole opere di carità al mantenimento delle condizioni esistenti, occorrerebbe creare un giusto ordine, nel quale tutti ricevano la loro parte dei beni del mondo e quindi non abbiano più bisogno delle opere di carità. In questa argomentazione, bisogna riconoscerlo, c'è del vero, ma anche non poco di errato. È vero che norma fondamentale dello Stato deve essere il perseguimento della giustizia e che lo scopo di un giusto ordine sociale è di garantire a ciascuno, nel rispetto del principio di sussidiarietà, la sua parte dei beni comuni. È quanto la dottrina cristiana sullo Stato e la dottrina sociale della Chiesa hanno sempre sottolineato. La questione del giusto ordine della collettività, da un punto di vista storico, è entrata in una nuova situazione con la formazione della società industriale nell'Ottocento. Il sorgere dell'industria moderna ha dissolto le vecchie strutture sociali e con la massa dei salariati ha provocato un cambiamento radicale nella composizione della società, all'interno della quale il rapporto tra capitale e lavoro è diventato la questione decisiva — una questione che sotto tale forma era prima sconosciuta. Le strutture di produzione e il capitale erano ormai il nuovo potere che, posto nelle mani di pochi, comportava per le masse lavoratrici una privazione di diritti contro la quale bisognava ribellarsi.

27. È doveroso ammettere che i rappresentanti della Chiesa hanno percepito solo lentamente che il problema della giusta struttura della società si poneva in modo nuovo. Non mancarono pionieri: uno di questi fu, ad esempio, il Vescovo

Ketteler di Magonza († 1877). Come risposta alle necessità concrete sorsero pure circoli, associazioni, unioni, federazioni e soprattutto nuove Congregazioni religiose, che nell'Ottocento scesero in campo contro la povertà, le malattie e le situazioni di carenza nel settore educativo. Nel 1891, entrò in scena il magistero pontificio con l'Enciclica *Rerum novarum* di Leone XIII. Vi fece seguito, nel 1931, l'Enciclica di Pio XI *Quadragesimo anno*. Il beato Papa Giovanni XXIII pubblicò, nel 1961, l'Enciclica *Mater et Magistra*, mentre Paolo VI nell'Enciclica *Populorum progressio* (1967) e nella Lettera apostolica *Octogesima adveniens* (1971) affrontò con insistenza la problematica sociale, che nel frattempo si era acutizzata soprattutto in America Latina. Il mio grande Predecessore Giovanni Paolo II ci ha lasciato una trilogia di Encicliche sociali: *Laborem exercens* (1981), *Sollicitudo rei socialis* (1987) e infine *Centesimus annus* (1991). Così nel confronto con situazioni e problemi sempre nuovi è venuta sviluppandosi una dottrina sociale cattolica, che nel 2004 è stata presentata in modo organico nel *Compendio della dottrina sociale della Chiesa*, redatto dal Pontificio Consiglio *Iustitia et Pax*. Il marxismo aveva indicato nella rivoluzione mondiale e nella sua preparazione la panacea per la problematica sociale: attraverso la rivoluzione e la conseguente collettivizzazione dei mezzi di produzione — si asseriva in tale dottrina — doveva improvvisamente andare tutto in modo diverso e migliore. Questo sogno è svanito. Nella situazione difficile nella quale oggi ci troviamo anche a causa della globalizzazione dell'economia, la dottrina sociale della Chiesa è diventata un'indicazione fondamentale, che propone orientamenti validi ben al di là dei confini di essa: questi orientamenti — di fronte al progredire dello sviluppo — devono essere affrontati nel dialogo con tutti coloro che si preoccupano seriamente dell'uomo e del suo mondo.

28. Per definire più accuratamente la relazione tra il necessario impegno per la giustizia e il servizio della carità, occorre prendere nota di due fondamentali situazioni di fatto:

a) Il giusto ordine della società e dello Stato è compito centrale della politica. Uno Stato che non fosse retto secondo giustizia si ridurrebbe ad una grande banda di ladri, come disse una volta Agostino: «*Remota itaque iustitia quid sunt*

regna nisi magna latrocinia?».[18] Alla struttura fondamentale del cristianesimo appartiene la distinzione tra ciò che è di Cesare e ciò che è di Dio (cfr
Mt 22, 21), cioè la distinzione tra Stato e Chiesa o,
come dice il Concilio Vaticano II, l'autonomia
delle realtà temporali.[19] Lo Stato non può imporre la religione, ma deve garantire la sua libertà e la
pace tra gli aderenti alle diverse religioni; la Chiesa come espressione sociale della fede cristiana,
da parte sua, ha la sua indipendenza e vive sulla
base della fede la sua forma comunitaria, che lo
Stato deve rispettare. Le due sfere sono distinte,
ma sempre in relazione reciproca.

La giustizia è lo scopo e quindi anche la misura intrinseca di ogni politica. La politica è più
che una semplice tecnica per la definizione dei
pubblici ordinamenti: la sua origine e il suo scopo
si trovano appunto nella giustizia, e questa è di
natura etica. Così lo Stato si trova di fatto inevi-
tabilmente di fronte all'interrogativo: come realizzare la giustizia qui ed ora? Ma questa domanda
presuppone l'altra più radicale: che cosa è la giu-

[18] *De Civitate Dei*, IV, 4: *CCL* 47, 102.
[19] Cfr Cost. past. sulla Chiesa nel mondo contempora-
neo *Gaudium et spes*, 36.

stizia? Questo è un problema che riguarda la ragione pratica; ma per poter operare rettamente, la ragione deve sempre di nuovo essere purificata, perché il suo accecamento etico, derivante dal prevalere dell'interesse e del potere che l'abbagliano, è un pericolo mai totalmente eliminabile.

In questo punto politica e fede si toccano. Senz'altro, la fede ha la sua specifica natura di incontro con il Dio vivente — un incontro che ci apre nuovi orizzonti molto al di là dell'ambito proprio della ragione. Ma al contempo essa è una forza purificatrice per la ragione stessa. Partendo dalla prospettiva di Dio, la libera dai suoi accecamenti e perciò l'aiuta ad essere meglio se stessa. La fede permette alla ragione di svolgere in modo migliore il suo compito e di vedere meglio ciò che le è proprio. È qui che si colloca la dottrina sociale cattolica: essa non vuole conferire alla Chiesa un potere sullo Stato. Neppure vuole imporre a coloro che non condividono la fede prospettive e modi di comportamento che appartengono a questa. Vuole semplicemente contribuire alla purificazione della ragione e recare il proprio aiuto per far sì che ciò che è giusto possa, qui ed ora, essere riconosciuto e poi anche realizzato.

La dottrina sociale della Chiesa argomenta a partire dalla ragione e dal diritto naturale, cioè a partire da ciò che è conforme alla natura di ogni essere umano. E sa che non è compito della Chiesa far essa stessa valere politicamente questa dottrina: essa vuole servire la formazione della coscienza nella politica e contribuire affinché cresca la percezione delle vere esigenze della giustizia e, insieme, la disponibilità ad agire in base ad esse, anche quando ciò contrastasse con situazioni di interesse personale. Questo significa che la costruzione di un giusto ordinamento sociale e statale, mediante il quale a ciascuno venga dato ciò che gli spetta, è un compito fondamentale che ogni generazione deve nuovamente affrontare. Trattandosi di un compito politico, questo non può essere incarico immediato della Chiesa. Ma siccome è allo stesso tempo un compito umano primario, la Chiesa ha il dovere di offrire attraverso la purificazione della ragione e attraverso la formazione etica il suo contributo specifico, affinché le esigenze della giustizia diventino comprensibili e politicamente realizzabili.

La Chiesa non può e non deve prendere nelle sue mani la battaglia politica per realizzare la società più giusta possibile. Non può e non deve mettersi al posto dello Stato. Ma non può e non deve neanche restare ai margini nella lotta per la giustizia. Deve inserirsi in essa per la via dell'argomentazione razionale e deve risvegliare le forze spirituali, senza le quali la giustizia, che sempre richiede anche rinunce, non può affermarsi e prosperare. La società giusta non può essere opera della Chiesa, ma deve essere realizzata dalla politica. Tuttavia l'adoperarsi per la giustizia lavorando per l'apertura dell'intelligenza e della volontà alle esigenze del bene la interessa profondamente.

b) L'amore — *caritas* — sarà sempre necessario, anche nella società più giusta. Non c'è nessun ordinamento statale giusto che possa rendere superfluo il servizio dell'amore. Chi vuole sbarazzarsi dell'amore si dispone a sbarazzarsi dell'uomo in quanto uomo. Ci sarà sempre sofferenza che necessita di consolazione e di aiuto. Sempre ci sarà solitudine. Sempre ci saranno anche situazioni di necessità materiale nelle quali è indispensabile un aiuto nella linea di un concreto amore per il prossimo.[20] Lo Stato che vuole provvedere a tutto, che assorbe tutto in sé, diventa in definitiva

---

[20] Cfr CONGREGAZIONE PER I VESCOVI, Direttorio per il ministero pastorale dei Vescovi *Apostolorum Successores* (22 febbraio 2004), 197, Città del Vaticano, 2004, 2ª, 209.

un'istanza burocratica che non può assicurare l'essenziale di cui l'uomo sofferente — ogni uomo — ha bisogno: l'amorevole dedizione personale. Non uno Stato che regoli e domini tutto è ciò che ci occorre, ma invece uno Stato che generosamente riconosca e sostenga, nella linea del principio di sussidiarietà, le iniziative che sorgono dalle diverse forze sociali e uniscono spontaneità e vicinanza agli uomini bisognosi di aiuto. La Chiesa è una di queste forze vive: in essa pulsa la dinamica dell'amore suscitato dallo Spirito di Cristo. Questo amore non offre agli uomini solamente un aiuto materiale, ma anche ristoro e cura dell'anima, un aiuto spesso più necessario del sostegno materiale. L'affermazione secondo la quale le strutture giuste renderebbero superflue le opere di carità di fatto nasconde una concezione materialistica dell'uomo: il pregiudizio secondo cui l'uomo vivrebbe «di solo pane» (*Mt* 4, 4; cfr *Dt* 8, 3) — convinzione che umilia l'uomo e disconosce proprio ciò che è più specificamente umano.

29. Così possiamo ora determinare più precisamente, nella vita della Chiesa, la relazione tra l'impegno per un giusto ordinamento dello Stato e della società, da una parte, e l'attività caritativa organizzata, dall'altra. Si è visto che la formazione di strutture giuste non è immediatamente compito della Chiesa, ma appartiene alla sfera della politica, cioè all'ambito della ragione autoresponsabile. In questo, il compito della Chiesa è mediato, in quanto le spetta di contribuire alla purificazione della ragione e al risveglio delle forze morali, senza le quali non vengono costruite strutture giuste, né queste possono essere operative a lungo.

Il compito immediato di operare per un giusto ordine nella società è invece proprio dei fedeli laici. Come cittadini dello Stato, essi sono chiamati a partecipare in prima persona alla vita pubblica. Non possono pertanto abdicare «alla molteplice e svariata azione economica, sociale, legislativa, amministrativa e culturale, destinata a promuovere organicamente e istituzionalmente *il bene comune*».[21] Missione dei fedeli laici è pertanto di configurare rettamente la vita sociale, rispet-

---

[21] GIOVANNI PAOLO II, Esort. ap. post-sinodale *Christifideles laici* (30 dicembre 1988), 42: *AAS* 81 (1989), 472.

tandone la legittima autonomia e cooperando con gli altri cittadini secondo le rispettive competenze e sotto la propria responsabilità.[22] Anche se le espressioni specifiche della carità ecclesiale non possono mai confondersi con l'attività dello Stato, resta tuttavia vero che la carità deve animare l'intera esistenza dei fedeli laici e quindi anche la loro attività politica, vissuta come «carità sociale».[23]

Le organizzazioni caritative della Chiesa costituiscono invece un suo *opus proprium*, un compito a lei congeniale, nel quale essa non collabora collateralmente, ma agisce come soggetto direttamente responsabile, facendo quello che corrisponde alla sua natura. La Chiesa non può mai essere dispensata dall'esercizio della carità come attività organizzata dei credenti e, d'altra parte, non ci sarà mai una situazione nella quale non occorra la carità di ciascun singolo cristiano, per-

[22] Cfr Congregazione per la Dottrina della Fede, *Nota dottrinale circa alcune questioni riguardanti l'impegno e il comportamento dei cattolici nella vita politica* (24 novembre 2002), 1: *L'Osservatore Romano,* 17 gennaio 2003, p. 6.

[23] *Catechismo della Chiesa Cattolica*, 1939.

ché l'uomo, al di là della giustizia, ha e avrà sempre bisogno dell'amore.

Le molteplici strutture di servizio caritativo nell'odierno contesto sociale

30. Prima di tentare una definizione del profilo specifico delle attività ecclesiali a servizio dell'uomo, vorrei ora considerare la situazione generale dell'impegno per la giustizia e per l'amore nel mondo odierno.

a) I mezzi di comunicazione di massa hanno oggi reso il nostro pianeta più piccolo, avvicinando velocemente uomini e culture profondamente diversi. Se questo « stare insieme » a volte suscita incomprensioni e tensioni, tuttavia, il fatto di venire, ora, in modo molto più immediato a conoscenza delle necessità degli uomini costituisce soprattutto un appello a condividerne la situazione e le difficoltà. Ogni giorno siamo resi coscienti di quanto si soffra nel mondo, nonostante i grandi progressi in campo scientifico e tecnico, a causa di una multiforme miseria, sia materiale che spirituale. Questo nostro tempo richiede, dunque, una nuova disponibilità a soccorrere il prossimo bisognoso. Già il Concilio Vaticano II lo ha sottolineato con parole molto chiare: «Oggi che i mezzi di comunicazione sono divenuti più rapidi e le distanze fra gli uomini quasi eliminate [...], l'azione caritativa può e deve abbracciare tutti assolutamente gli uomini e tutte quante le necessità».[24]

D'altro canto — ed è questo un aspetto provocatorio e al contempo incoraggiante del processo di globalizzazione — il presente mette a nostra disposizione innumerevoli strumenti per prestare aiuto umanitario ai fratelli bisognosi, non ultimi i moderni sistemi per la distribuzione di cibo e di vestiario, come anche per l'offerta di alloggio e di accoglienza. Superando i confini delle comunità nazionali, la sollecitudine per il prossimo tende così ad allargare i suoi orizzonti al mondo intero. Il Concilio Vaticano II ha giustamente rilevato: «Tra i segni del nostro tempo è degno di speciale menzione il crescente e inarrestabile senso di solidarietà di tutti i popoli».[25] Gli enti dello Stato e le associazioni umanitarie asse-

---

[24] Decr. sull'apostolato dei laici *Apostolicam actuositatem*, 8.
[25] *Ibid.*, 14.

condano iniziative volte a questo scopo, per lo più attraverso sussidi o sgravi fiscali, gli uni, rendendo disponibili considerevoli risorse, le altre. In tal modo la solidarietà espressa dalla società civile supera significativamente quella dei singoli.

b) In questa situazione sono nate e cresciute, tra le istanze statali ed ecclesiali, numerose forme di collaborazione che si sono rivelate fruttuose. Le istanze ecclesiali, con la trasparenza del loro operare e la fedeltà al dovere di testimoniare l'amore, potranno animare cristianamente anche le istanze civili, favorendo un coordinamento vicendevole che non mancherà di giovare all'efficacia del servizio caritativo.[26] Si sono pure formate, in questo contesto, molteplici organizzazioni con scopi caritativi o filantropici, che si impegnano per raggiungere, nei confronti dei problemi sociali e politici esistenti, soluzioni soddisfacenti sotto l'aspetto umanitario. Un fenomeno importante del nostro tempo è il sorgere e il diffondersi di diverse forme di volontariato, che si fanno carico di

[26] Cfr Congregazione per i Vescovi, Direttorio per il ministero pastorale dei Vescovi *Apostolorum Successores* (22 febbraio 2004), 195: Città del Vaticano 2004, 2ª, 206-208.

una molteplicità di servizi.[27] Vorrei qui indirizzare una particolare parola di apprezzamento e di ringraziamento a tutti coloro che partecipano in vario modo a queste attività. Tale impegno diffuso costituisce per i giovani una scuola di vita che educa alla solidarietà e alla disponibilità a dare non semplicemente qualcosa, ma se stessi. All'anti-cultura della morte, che si esprime per esempio nella droga, si contrappone così l'amore che non cerca se stesso, ma che, proprio nella disponibilità a «perdere se stesso» per l'altro (cfr *Lc* 17, 33 e par.), si rivela come cultura della vita.

Anche nella Chiesa cattolica e in altre Chiese e Comunità ecclesiali sono sorte nuove forme di attività caritativa, e ne sono riapparse di antiche con slancio rinnovato. Sono forme nelle quali si riesce spesso a costituire un felice legame tra evangelizzazione e opere di carità. Desidero qui confermare esplicitamente quello che il mio grande Predecessore Giovanni Paolo II ha scritto nella sua Enciclica *Sollicitudo rei socialis,*[28] quando ha

---

[27] Cfr GIOVANNI PAOLO II, Esort. ap. post sinodale *Christifideles laici* (30 dicembre 1988), 41: *AAS* 81 (1989), 470-472.

[28] Cfr n. 32: *AAS* 80 (1988), 556.

dichiarato la disponibilità della Chiesa cattolica a collaborare con le Organizzazioni caritative di queste Chiese e Comunità, poiché noi tutti siamo mossi dalla medesima motivazione fondamentale e abbiamo davanti agli occhi il medesimo scopo: un vero umanesimo, che riconosce nell'uomo l'immagine di Dio e vuole aiutarlo a realizzare una vita conforme a questa dignità. L'Enciclica *Ut unum sint* ha poi ancora una volta sottolineato che, per uno sviluppo del mondo verso il meglio, è necessaria la voce comune dei cristiani, il loro impegno «per il rispetto dei diritti e dei bisogni di tutti, specie dei poveri, degli umiliati e degli indifesi».[29] Vorrei qui esprimere la mia gioia per il fatto che questo desiderio abbia trovato in tutto il mondo una larga eco in numerose iniziative.

Il profilo specifico dell'attività caritativa della Chiesa

31. L'aumento di organizzazioni diversificate, che si impegnano per l'uomo nelle sue svariate necessità, si spiega in fondo col fatto che l'impe-

---

[29] N. 43: *AAS* 87 (1995), 946.

rativo dell'amore del prossimo è iscritto dal Creatore nella stessa natura dell'uomo. Tale crescita, però, è anche un effetto della presenza nel mondo del cristianesimo, che sempre di nuovo risveglia e rende efficace questo imperativo, spesso profondamente oscurato nel corso della storia. La riforma del paganesimo, tentata dall'imperatore Giuliano l'Apostata, è solo un esempio iniziale di una simile efficacia. In questo senso, la forza del cristianesimo si espande ben oltre le frontiere della fede cristiana. È perciò molto importante che l'attività caritativa della Chiesa mantenga tutto il suo splendore e non si dissolva nella comune organizzazione assistenziale, diventandone una semplice variante. Ma quali sono, ora, gli elementi costitutivi che formano l'essenza della carità cristiana ed ecclesiale?

a) Secondo il modello offerto dalla parabola del buon Samaritano, la carità cristiana è dapprima semplicemente la risposta a ciò che, in una determinata situazione, costituisce la necessità immediata: gli affamati devono essere saziati, i nudi vestiti, i malati curati in vista della guarigione, i carcerati visitati, ecc. Le Organizzazioni caritative della Chiesa, a cominciare da quelle della

Caritas (diocesana, nazionale, internazionale), devono fare il possibile, affinché siano disponibili i relativi mezzi e soprattutto gli uomini e le donne che assumano tali compiti. Per quanto riguarda il servizio che le persone svolgono per i sofferenti, occorre innanzitutto la competenza professionale: i soccorritori devono essere formati in modo da saper fare la cosa giusta nel modo giusto, assumendo poi l'impegno del proseguimento della cura. La competenza professionale è una prima fondamentale necessità, ma da sola non basta. Si tratta, infatti, di esseri umani, e gli esseri umani necessitano sempre di qualcosa in più di una cura solo tecnicamente corretta. Hanno bisogno di umanità. Hanno bisogno dell'attenzione del cuore. Quanti operano nelle Istituzioni caritative della Chiesa devono distinguersi per il fatto che non si limitano ad eseguire in modo abile la cosa conveniente al momento, ma si dedicano all'altro con le attenzioni suggerite dal cuore, in modo che questi sperimenti la loro ricchezza di umanità. Perciò, oltre alla preparazione professionale, a tali operatori è necessaria anche, e soprattutto, la « formazione del cuore »: occorre condurli a quell'incontro con Dio in Cristo che susciti in loro l'amore e apra il loro animo all'altro, così che per loro l'amore del prossimo non sia più un comandamento imposto per così dire dall'esterno, ma una conseguenza derivante dalla loro fede che diventa operante nell'amore (cfr *Gal* 5, 6).

b) L'attività caritativa cristiana deve essere indipendente da partiti ed ideologie. Non è un mezzo per cambiare il mondo in modo ideologico e non sta al servizio di strategie mondane, ma è attualizzazione qui ed ora dell'amore di cui l'uomo ha sempre bisogno. Il tempo moderno, soprattutto a partire dall'Ottocento, è dominato da diverse varianti di una filosofia del progresso, la cui forma più radicale è il marxismo. Parte della strategia marxista è la teoria dell'impoverimento: chi in una situazione di potere ingiusto — essa sostiene — aiuta l'uomo con iniziative di carità, si pone di fatto a servizio di quel sistema di ingiustizia, facendolo apparire, almeno fino a un certo punto, sopportabile. Viene così frenato il potenziale rivoluzionario e quindi bloccato il rivolgimento verso un mondo migliore. Perciò la carità viene contestata ed attaccata come sistema di conservazione dello *status quo*. In realtà, questa è una filosofia disumana. L'uomo che vive nel presente viene sacrificato al *moloch* del futuro — un futuro la cui effettiva realizzazione rimane almeno dubbia. In verità, l'umanizzazione del mondo non può essere promossa rinunciando, per il momento, a comportarsi in modo umano. Ad un mondo migliore si contribuisce soltanto facendo il bene adesso ed in prima persona, con passione e ovunque ce ne sia la possibilità, indipendentemente da strategie e programmi di partito. Il programma del cristiano — il programma del buon Samaritano, il programma di Gesù — è «un cuore che vede». Questo cuore vede dove c'è bisogno di amore e agisce in modo conseguente. Ovviamente alla spontaneità del singolo deve aggiungersi, quando l'attività caritativa è assunta dalla Chiesa come iniziativa comunitaria, anche la programmazione, la previdenza, la collaborazione con altre istituzioni simili.

c) La carità, inoltre, non deve essere un mezzo in funzione di ciò che oggi viene indicato come proselitismo. L'amore è gratuito; non viene esercitato per raggiungere altri scopi.[30] Ma questo non

---

[30] Cfr Congregazione per i Vescovi, Direttorio per il ministero pastorale dei Vescovi *Apostolorum Successores* (22 febbraio 2004), 196: Città del Vaticano 2004, 2ª, 208.

significa che l'azione caritativa debba, per così dire, lasciare Dio e Cristo da parte. È in gioco sempre tutto l'uomo. Spesso è proprio l'assenza di Dio la radice più profonda della sofferenza. Chi esercita la carità in nome della Chiesa non cercherà mai di imporre agli altri la fede della Chiesa. Egli sa che l'amore nella sua purezza e nella sua gratuità è la miglior testimonianza del Dio nel quale crediamo e dal quale siamo spinti ad amare. Il cristiano sa quando è tempo di parlare di Dio e quando è giusto tacere di Lui e lasciar parlare solamente l'amore. Egli sa che Dio è amore (cfr *1 Gv* 4, 8) e si rende presente proprio nei momenti in cui nient'altro viene fatto fuorché amare. Egli sa — per tornare alle domande di prima –, che il vilipendio dell'amore è vilipendio di Dio e dell'uomo, è il tentativo di fare a meno di Dio. Di conseguenza, la miglior difesa di Dio e dell'uomo consiste proprio nell'amore. È compito delle Organizzazioni caritative della Chiesa rafforzare questa consapevolezza nei propri membri, in modo che attraverso il loro agire — come attraverso il loro parlare, il loro tacere, il loro esempio — diventino testimoni credibili di Cristo.

I responsabili dell'azione caritativa della Chiesa

32. Infine, dobbiamo rivolgere ancora la nostra attenzione ai già citati responsabili dell'azione caritativa della Chiesa. Nelle precedenti riflessioni è ormai risultato chiaro che il vero soggetto delle varie Organizzazioni cattoliche che svolgono un servizio di carità è la Chiesa stessa — e ciò a tutti i livelli, iniziando dalle parrocchie, attraverso le Chiese particolari, fino alla Chiesa universale. Per questo è stato quanto mai opportuno che il mio venerato Predecessore Paolo VI abbia istituito il Pontificio Consiglio *Cor unum* quale istanza della Santa Sede responsabile per l'orientamento e il coordinamento tra le organizzazioni e le attività caritative promosse dalla Chiesa cattolica. Alla struttura episcopale della Chiesa, poi, corrisponde il fatto che, nelle Chiese particolari, i Vescovi quali successori degli Apostoli portino la prima responsabilità della realizzazione, anche nel presente, del programma indicato negli *Atti degli Apostoli* (cfr 2, 42-44): la Chiesa in quanto famiglia di Dio deve essere, oggi come ieri, un luogo di aiuto vicendevole e al contempo un luogo di disponibilità a servire anche coloro che, fuori di essa, hanno bisogno di aiuto. Durante il rito dell'Ordinazione episcopale, il vero e proprio atto di consacrazione è preceduto da alcune domande al candidato, nelle quali sono espressi gli elementi essenziali del suo ufficio e gli vengono ricordati i doveri del suo futuro ministero. In questo contesto l'ordinando promette espressamente di essere, nel nome del Signore, accogliente e misericordioso verso i poveri e verso tutti i bisognosi di conforto e di aiuto.[31] Il *Codice di Diritto Canonico*, nei canoni riguardanti il ministero episcopale, non tratta espressamente della carità come di uno specifico ambito dell'attività episcopale, ma parla solo in modo generale del compito del Vescovo, che è quello di coordinare le diverse opere di apostolato nel rispetto della loro propria indole.[32] Recentemente, tuttavia, il *Direttorio per il ministero pastorale dei Vescovi* ha approfondito più concretamente il dovere della carità come compito intrinseco della Chiesa inte-

[31] Cfr PONTIFICALE ROMANUM, *De ordinatione episcopi*, 43.
[32] Cfr can. 394; *Codice dei Canoni delle Chiese Orientali*, can. 203.

ra e del Vescovo nella sua Diocesi[33] ed ha sottolineato che l'esercizio della carità è un atto della Chiesa come tale e che, così come il servizio della Parola e dei Sacramenti, fa parte anch'esso dell'essenza della sua missione originaria.[34]

33. Per quanto concerne i collaboratori che svolgono sul piano pratico il lavoro della carità nella Chiesa, l'essenziale è già stato detto: essi non devono ispirarsi alle ideologie del miglioramento del mondo, ma farsi guidare dalla fede che nell'amore diventa operante (cfr *Gal* 5, 6). Devono essere quindi persone mosse innanzitutto dall'amore di Cristo, persone il cui cuore Cristo ha conquistato col suo amore, risvegliandovi l'amore per il prossimo. Il criterio ispiratore del loro agire dovrebbe essere l'affermazione presente nella *Seconda Lettera ai Corinzi*: «L'amore del Cristo ci spinge» (5, 14). La consapevolezza che in Lui Dio stesso si è donato per noi fino alla morte deve indurci a non vivere più per noi stessi, ma per Lui, e con Lui per gli altri. Chi ama Cristo

---

[33] Cfr nn. 193-198, 204-210.
[34] Cfr *ibid.*, 194, 205-206.

ama la Chiesa e vuole che essa sia sempre più espressione e strumento dell'amore che da Lui promana. Il collaboratore di ogni Organizzazione caritativa cattolica vuole lavorare con la Chiesa e quindi col Vescovo, affinché l'amore di Dio si diffonda nel mondo. Attraverso la sua partecipazione all'esercizio dell'amore della Chiesa, egli vuole essere testimone di Dio e di Cristo e proprio per questo vuole fare del bene agli uomini gratuitamente.

34. L'apertura interiore alla dimensione cattolica della Chiesa non potrà non disporre il collaboratore a sintonizzarsi con le altre Organizzazioni nel servizio alle varie forme di bisogno; ciò tuttavia dovrà avvenire nel rispetto del profilo specifico del servizio richiesto da Cristo ai suoi discepoli. San Paolo nel suo inno alla carità (cfr *1 Cor* 13) ci insegna che la carità è sempre più che semplice attività: «Se anche distribuissi tutte le mie sostanze e dessi il mio corpo per essere bruciato, ma non avessi la carità, niente mi giova» (v. 3). Questo inno deve essere la *Magna Carta* dell'intero servizio ecclesiale; in esso sono riassunte tutte le riflessioni che, nel corso di questa

Lettera enciclica, ho svolto sull'amore. L'azione pratica resta insufficiente se in essa non si rende percepibile l'amore per l'uomo, un amore che si nutre dell'incontro con Cristo. L'intima partecipazione personale al bisogno e alla sofferenza dell'altro diventa così un partecipargli me stesso: perché il dono non umilii l'altro, devo dargli non soltanto qualcosa di mio ma me stesso, devo essere presente nel dono come persona.

35. Questo giusto modo di servire rende l'operatore umile. Egli non assume una posizione di superiorità di fronte all'altro, per quanto misera possa essere sul momento la sua situazione. Cristo ha preso l'ultimo posto nel mondo — la croce — e proprio con questa umiltà radicale ci ha redenti e costantemente ci aiuta. Chi è in condizione di aiutare riconosce che proprio in questo modo viene aiutato anche lui; non è suo merito né titolo di vanto il fatto di poter aiutare. Questo compito è grazia. Quanto più uno s'adopera per gli altri, tanto più capirà e farà sua la parola di Cristo: «Siamo servi inutili» (*Lc* 17, 10). Egli riconosce infatti di agire non in base ad una superiorità o maggior efficienza personale, ma perché il Signore gliene fa dono. A volte l'eccesso del bisogno e i limiti del proprio operare potranno esporlo alla tentazione dello scoraggiamento. Ma proprio allora gli sarà d'aiuto il sapere che, in definitiva, egli non è che uno strumento nelle mani del Signore; si libererà così dalla presunzione di dover realizzare, in prima persona e da solo, il necessario miglioramento del mondo. In umiltà farà quello che gli è possibile fare e in umiltà affiderà il resto al Signore. È Dio che governa il mondo, non noi. Noi gli prestiamo il nostro servizio solo per quello che possiamo e finché Egli ce ne dà la forza. Fare, però, quanto ci è possibile con la forza di cui disponiamo, questo è il compito che mantiene il buon servo di Gesù Cristo sempre in movimento: «L'amore del Cristo ci spinge» (*2 Cor* 5, 14).

36. L'esperienza della smisuratezza del bisogno può, da un lato, spingerci nell'ideologia che pretende di fare ora quello che il governo del mondo da parte di Dio, a quanto pare, non consegue: la soluzione universale di ogni problema. Dall'altro lato, essa può diventare tentazione all'inerzia sulla base dell'impressione che, comunque, nulla possa essere realizzato. In questa situazione il contatto vivo con Cristo è l'aiuto decisivo per restare sulla retta via: né cadere in una superbia che disprezza l'uomo e non costruisce in realtà nulla, ma piuttosto distrugge, né abbandonarsi alla rassegnazione che impedirebbe di lasciarsi guidare dall'amore e così servire l'uomo. La preghiera come mezzo per attingere sempre di nuovo forza da Cristo, diventa qui un'urgenza del tutto concreta. Chi prega non spreca il suo tempo, anche se la situazione ha tutte le caratteristiche dell'emergenza e sembra spingere unicamente all'azione. La pietà non indebolisce la lotta contro la povertà o addirittura contro la miseria del prossimo. La beata Teresa di Calcutta è un esempio molto evidente del fatto che il tempo dedicato a Dio nella preghiera non solo non nuoce all'efficacia ed all'operosità dell'amore verso il prossimo, ma ne è in realtà l'inesauribile sorgente. Nella sua lettera per la Quaresima del 1996 la beata scriveva ai suoi collaboratori laici: «Noi abbiamo bisogno di questo intimo legame con Dio nella nostra vita quotidiana. E come possiamo ottenerlo? Attraverso la preghiera».

37. È venuto il momento di riaffermare l'importanza della preghiera di fronte all'attivismo e all'incombente secolarismo di molti cristiani impegnati nel lavoro caritativo. Ovviamente, il cristiano che prega non pretende di cambiare i piani di Dio o di correggere quanto Dio ha previsto. Egli cerca piuttosto l'incontro con il Padre di Gesù Cristo, chiedendo che Egli sia presente con il conforto del suo Spirito in lui e nella sua opera. La familiarità col Dio personale e l'abbandono alla sua volontà impediscono il degrado dell'uomo, lo salvano dalla prigionia di dottrine fanatiche e terroristiche. Un atteggiamento autenticamente religioso evita che l'uomo si eriga a giudice di Dio, accusandolo di permettere la miseria senza provar compassione per le sue creature. Ma chi pretende di lottare contro Dio facendo leva sull'interesse dell'uomo, su chi potrà contare quando l'azione umana si dimostrerà impotente?

38. Certo Giobbe può lamentarsi di fronte a Dio per la sofferenza incomprensibile, e apparentemente ingiustificabile, presente nel mondo. Così egli parla nel suo dolore: «Oh, potessi sapere dove trovarlo, potessi arrivare fino al suo trono! ... Verrei a sapere le parole che mi risponde e capirei che cosa mi deve dire. Con sfoggio di potenza discuterebbe con me? ... Per questo davanti a lui sono atterrito, ci penso ed ho paura di lui. Dio ha fiaccato il mio cuore, l'Onnipotente mi ha atterrito» (23, 3. 5-6. 15-16). Spesso non ci è dato di conoscere il motivo per cui Dio trattiene il suo braccio invece di intervenire. Del resto, Egli neppure ci impedisce di gridare, come Gesù in croce: «Dio mio, Dio mio, perché mi hai abbandonato?» (*Mt* 27, 46). Noi dovremmo rimanere con questa domanda di fronte al suo volto, in dialogo orante: «Fino a quando esiterai ancora, Signore, tu che sei santo e verace?» (*Ap* 6, 10). È sant'Agostino che dà a questa nostra sofferenza la risposta della fede: «*Si comprehendis, non est Deus*» — Se tu lo comprendi, allora non è Dio.[35] La nostra protesta non vuole sfidare Dio, né insinuare la presenza in Lui di errore, debolezza o indifferenza. Per il credente non è possibile pensare che Egli sia impotente, oppure che «stia dormendo» (cfr *1 Re* 18, 27). Piuttosto è vero che perfino

[35] *Sermo* 52, 16: *PL* 38, 360.

il nostro gridare è, come sulla bocca di Gesù in croce, il modo estremo e più profondo per affermare la nostra fede nella sua sovrana potestà. I cristiani infatti continuano a credere, malgrado tutte le incomprensioni e confusioni del mondo circostante, nella «bontà di Dio» e nel «suo amore per gli uomini» (*Tt* 3, 4). Essi, pur immersi come gli altri uomini nella drammatica complessità delle vicende della storia, rimangono saldi nella certezza che Dio è Padre e ci ama, anche se il suo silenzio rimane incomprensibile per noi.

39. Fede, speranza e carità vanno insieme. La speranza si articola praticamente nella virtù della pazienza, che non vien meno nel bene neanche di fronte all'apparente insuccesso, ed in quella dell'umiltà, che accetta il mistero di Dio e si fida di Lui anche nell'oscurità. La fede ci mostra il Dio che ha dato il suo Figlio per noi e suscita così in noi la vittoriosa certezza che è proprio vero: Dio è amore! In questo modo essa trasforma la nostra impazienza e i nostri dubbi nella sicura speranza che Dio tiene il mondo nelle sue mani e che nonostante ogni oscurità Egli vince, come mediante le sue immagini sconvolgenti alla fine l'*Apocalisse* mostra in modo radioso. La fede, che prende coscienza dell'amore di Dio rivelatosi nel cuore trafitto di Gesù sulla croce, suscita a sua volta l'amore. Esso è la luce — in fondo l'unica — che rischiara sempre di nuovo un mondo buio e ci dà il coraggio di vivere e di agire. L'amore è possibile, e noi siamo in grado di praticarlo perché creati ad immagine di Dio. Vivere l'amore e in questo modo far entrare la luce di Dio nel mondo, ecco ciò a cui vorrei invitare con la presente Enciclica.

CONCLUSIONE

40. Guardiamo infine ai Santi, a coloro che hanno esercitato in modo esemplare la carità. Il pensiero va, in particolare, a Martino di Tours († 397), prima soldato poi monaco e vescovo: quasi come un'icona, egli mostra il valore insostituibile della testimonianza individuale della carità. Alle porte di Amiens, Martino fa a metà del suo mantello con un povero: Gesù stesso, nella notte, gli appare in sogno rivestito di quel mantello, a confermare la validità perenne della parola evangelica: «Ero nudo e mi avete vestito ... Ogni volta che avete fatto queste cose a uno solo di questi miei fratelli più piccoli, l'avete fatto a me» (*Mt* 25, 36. 40).[36] Ma nella storia della Chiesa, quante altre testimonianze di carità possono essere citate! In particolare tutto il movimento mo-

---

[36] Cfr SULPICIO SEVERO, *Vita Sancti Martini*, 3, 1-3: *SCh* 133, 256-258.

nastico, fin dai suoi inizi con sant'Antonio abate (†356), esprime un ingente servizio di carità verso il prossimo. Nel confronto «faccia a faccia» con quel Dio che è Amore, il monaco avverte l'esigenza impellente di trasformare in servizio del prossimo, oltre che di Dio, tutta la propria vita. Si spiegano così le grandi strutture di accoglienza, di ricovero e di cura sorte accanto ai monasteri. Si spiegano pure le ingenti iniziative di promozione umana e di formazione cristiana, destinate innanzitutto ai più poveri, di cui si sono fatti carico dapprima gli Ordini monastici e mendicanti e poi i vari Istituti religiosi maschili e femminili, lungo tutta la storia della Chiesa. Figure di Santi come Francesco d'Assisi, Ignazio di Loyola, Giovanni di Dio, Camillo de Lellis, Vincenzo de' Paoli, Luisa de Marillac, Giuseppe B. Cottolengo, Giovanni Bosco, Luigi Orione, Teresa di Calcutta — per fare solo alcuni nomi — rimangono modelli insigni di carità sociale per tutti gli uomini di buona volontà. I santi sono i veri portatori di luce all'interno della storia, perché sono uomini e donne di fede, di speranza e di amore.

41. Tra i santi eccelle Maria, Madre del Signore e specchio di ogni santità. Nel *Vangelo di Luca* la troviamo impegnata in un servizio di carità alla cugina Elisabetta, presso la quale resta «circa tre mesi» (1, 56) per assisterla nella fase terminale della gravidanza. «*Magnificat anima mea Dominum*», dice in occasione di questa visita — «L'anima mia rende grande il Signore» — (*Lc* 1, 46), ed esprime con ciò tutto il programma della sua vita: non mettere se stessa al centro, ma fare spazio a Dio incontrato sia nella preghiera che nel servizio al prossimo — solo allora il mondo diventa buono. Maria è grande proprio perché non vuole rendere grande se stessa, ma Dio. Ella è umile: non vuole essere nient'altro che l'ancella del Signore (cfr *Lc* 1, 38. 48). Ella sa di contribuire alla salvezza del mondo non compiendo una sua opera, ma solo mettendosi a piena disposizione delle iniziative di Dio. È una donna di speranza: solo perché crede alle promesse di Dio e attende la salvezza di Israele, l'angelo può venire da lei e chiamarla al servizio decisivo di queste promesse. Essa è una donna di fede: «Beata sei tu che hai creduto», le dice Elisabetta (cfr *Lc* 1, 45). Il *Magnificat* — un ritratto, per così dire, della sua anima — è interamente tessuto di fili della Sacra Scrittura, di fili tratti dalla Parola di Dio. Così si rivela che lei nella Parola di Dio è veramente a casa sua, ne esce e vi rientra con naturalezza. Ella parla e pensa con la Parola di Dio; la Parola di Dio diventa parola sua, e la sua parola nasce dalla Parola di Dio. Così si rivela, inoltre, che i suoi pensieri sono in sintonia con i pensieri di Dio, che il suo volere è un volere insieme con Dio. Essendo intimamente penetrata dalla Parola di Dio, ella può diventare madre della Parola incarnata. Infine, Maria è una donna che ama. Come potrebbe essere diversamente? In quanto credente che nella fede pensa con i pensieri di Dio e vuole con la volontà di Dio, ella non può essere che una donna che ama. Noi lo intuiamo nei gesti silenziosi, di cui ci riferiscono i racconti evangelici dell'infanzia. Lo vediamo nella delicatezza, con la quale a Cana percepisce la necessità in cui versano gli sposi e la presenta a Gesù. Lo vediamo nell'umiltà con cui accetta di essere trascurata nel periodo della vita pubblica di Gesù, sapendo che il Figlio deve fondare una nuova famiglia e che l'ora della Madre arriverà soltanto nel momento della croce, che sarà la vera ora di Gesù (cfr *Gv* 2, 4; 13, 1). Allora, quando i discepoli saranno fuggiti, lei resterà sotto la croce (cfr *Gv* 19, 25-27); più tardi, nell'ora di Pentecoste, saranno loro a stringersi intorno a lei nell'attesa dello Spirito Santo (cfr *At* 1, 14).

42.   Alla vita dei Santi non appartiene solo la loro biografia terrena, ma anche il loro vivere ed operare in Dio dopo la morte. Nei Santi diventa ovvio: chi va verso Dio non si allontana dagli uomini, ma si rende invece ad essi veramente vicino. In nessuno lo vediamo meglio che in Maria. La parola del Crocifisso al discepolo — a Giovanni e attraverso di lui a tutti i discepoli di Gesù: «Ecco tua madre» (*Gv* 19, 27) — diventa nel corso delle generazioni sempre nuovamente vera. Maria è diventata, di fatto, Madre di tutti i credenti. Alla sua bontà materna, come alla sua purezza e bellezza verginale, si rivolgono gli uomini di tutti i tempi e di tutte le parti del mondo nelle loro necessità e speranze, nelle loro gioie e sofferenze, nelle loro solitudini come anche nella condivisione comunitaria. E sempre sperimentano il dono della sua bontà, sperimentano l'amore inesauribile che ella riversa dal profondo del suo cuore. Le testimonianze di gratitudine, a lei tributate in tutti i continenti e in tutte le culture, sono il riconoscimento di quell'amore puro che non cerca se stesso, ma semplicemente vuole il bene. La devozione dei fedeli mostra, al contempo, l'intuizione infallibile di come un tale amore sia possibile: lo diventa grazie alla più intima unione con Dio, in virtù della quale si è totalmente pervasi da Lui — una condizione che permette a chi ha bevuto alla fonte dell'amore di Dio di diventare egli stesso una sorgente «da cui sgorgano fiumi di acqua viva» (cfr *Gv* 7, 38). Maria, la Vergine, la Madre, ci mostra che cos'è l'amore e da dove esso trae la sua origine, la sua forza sempre rinnovata. A lei affidiamo la Chiesa, la sua missione a servizio dell'amore:

> Santa Maria, Madre di Dio,
> tu hai donato al mondo la vera luce,
> Gesù, tuo Figlio — Figlio di Dio.
> Ti sei consegnata completamente
> alla chiamata di Dio
> e sei così diventata sorgente
> della bontà che sgorga da Lui.

Mostraci Gesù. Guidaci a Lui.
Insegnaci a conoscerlo e ad amarlo,
perché possiamo anche noi
diventare capaci di vero amore
ed essere sorgenti di acqua viva
in mezzo a un mondo assetato.

Dato a Roma, presso San Pietro, il 25 dicembre, solennità del Natale del Signore, dell'anno 2005, primo di Pontificato.

Benedictus PP XVI

INDICE

DIANA CHASE

Fremantle Arts Centre Press

Australia's finest small publisher

First published 2003 by
FREMANTLE ARTS CENTRE PRESS
25 Quarry Street, Fremantle
(PO Box 158, North Fremantle 6159)
Western Australia.
www.facp.iinet.net.au

Consultant Editor Alwyn Evans.
Production Coordinator Vanessa Bradley.
Cover Designer Marion Duke.
Typeset by Fremantle Arts Centre Press.
Printed by Griffin Press.

National Library of Australia
Cataloguing-in-publication data

    Chase, Diana.
    The lighthouse kids.

    For young adults.
    ISBN 1 86368 346 1.

    I. Title.

    A823.3

  The State of Western Australia has made an
investment in this project through ArtsWA in
association with the Lotteries Commission.

To Chris,
and all who love the sea

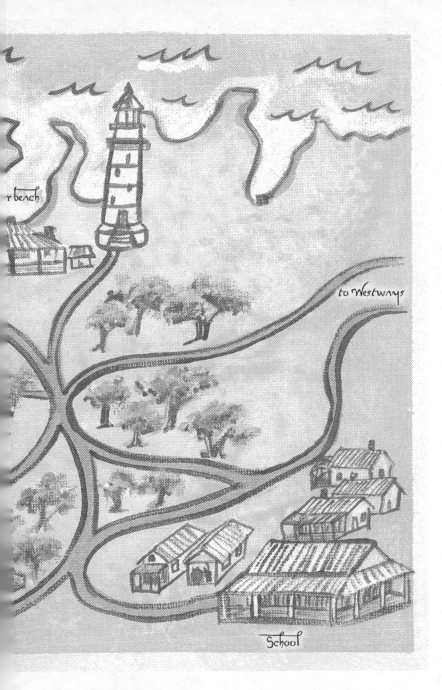

Many ships were lost on the lonely and uncharted reefs
of the Great South Land.
And what of those who struggled ashore?
Did they survive? How did they live? Did they wait,
watching the sea for a ship that never came?

1

The bus shuddered to a stop in a cloud of dust. Ellie held Davey's hand tightly and squinted through the windows to the glare outside. She cleared her throat. 'Is this it?' she whispered, her eyes finding Mrs Opie across the aisle.

Mrs Opie craned her neck to peer past the driver. 'Yes, look. It says Larsen's Point.' She rose, chanting, 'Oh I do like to be beside the sea-ea side, we'll soon be down beside the sea …'

Ellie flushed and glanced at the other passengers. She half-stood in the cramped seat space, peering past a loveheart and 'DP' scratched into the window. Beside her Davey squirmed and muttered, 'I gotta go.'

The bus driver stood. 'Larsen's Point,' he announced. 'And a tea break.' He climbed out of his seat, smiling at Ellie. 'Your stop, love. I'll get your things.'

'C'mon Davey.' Ellie pulled her brother to his feet and pushed him into his jacket. 'We get off now.' She brushed at her jeans and pulled at the scrunchy on her ponytail. 'C'mon,' she said again, nudging him into the aisle, ignoring his scared eyes and her own churning stomach.

Davey scowled. He leaned back, resisting. 'I gotta go,' he repeated.

Ellie rolled her eyes and sighed. 'Well come on then, dummy. You can't go in the bus.'

Mrs Opie clambered down the step after them and peered round the few scattered buildings. 'Larsen's Point, eh? Where is everyone?' The driver was burrowing through the luggage compartment on the underside of the bus. She poked him in the ribs. 'The stop's empty. There's no sign of their grandpop.'

The man glanced up and grinned patiently. 'He'll be here, love,' he said.

Other travellers fumbled their way off the bus.

Davey jiggled and pulled at Ellie's sleeve. 'Ellie! Now!' he repeated.

'Okay, ok-aayy.' She checked the terminal for 'Rest Room' signs. 'Down there,' she muttered, and Davey scuttled off.

The bus driver dumped their battered green duffle bags on the footpath and glanced down an empty track towards the headland. He scratched his nose. 'Your grandpa Hamish McCleod — the lighthouse keeper?'

Ellie nodded.

He grinned at her. 'Yeah, I know him — good bloke. Don't you worry love. He'll be along directly. Sometimes the track gets blocked, and today we're a tad early.'

Relieved, Ellie mumbled her thanks, wrinkling her eyes against the glare of sand and space. A fresh breeze flicked at her hair bringing with it the smell of the sea. She glanced upwards at wind-tossed clouds and bright blue sky. It was so different from the hard summer whiteness and red, baking earth of the north. And it wasn't even hot — not after Shelley.

A young woman came out of the Tourist Centre next to the bus stop. 'Eleanor and David Flannagan?'

'That's right.' Mrs Opie pushed Ellie forward.

The young woman smiled brightly. 'I'm Rica Tori, Tourist Centre manager. The road truck has just called in. There's a tree across the track and you are to wait here until your grandfather arrives.'

Ellie nodded and murmured, 'Thanks.' She wished the fluttering inside her would go away — that strangers didn't have to be part of her problems.

The bus driver checked in and collected numbers

for the return journey. He came out smiling at Ellie. 'You staying then? You okay?'

Ellie nodded. He patted her clumsily on the head, 'Good kid,' and climbed into his seat. 'Time to move, folks,' he called. 'All aboard!'

The other passengers straggled out of the coffee shop. A girl flicked her long brown hair back from her face and smiled vaguely at Ellie. Davey reappeared, tucking his shirt into his shorts.

Mrs Opie swooped on him, fussing with his collar. 'Oh my poor, sweet little man!' Davey squirmed and pulled away. Tears filled the woman's eyes. 'It's time to go and not a sign of that grandpop of yours.' She glared at the bus driver, 'I have to watch out for them, and their grandpop's still not here.'

The driver repeated his smile, and promised, 'Hamish McCleod will come.' He'd coped with anxious old ladies before.

Mrs Opie was unconvinced. 'Men!' she snorted and puffed out her cheeks. 'It's not right. Leaving poor motherless mites on their own! I'll have to wait and catch another bus.'

Ms Tori came forward. 'There's not another one till Wednesday, Ma'am. The children will be fine with me.'

Ellie took the older woman's arm, moving her

towards the bus. 'We'll be fine, Mrs Opie. Honest. You'd better get on. They're ready to go and your sister's waiting.'

With sounds of outrage and protest, Mrs Opie heaved herself up the step. She took a deep breath. 'You've got my sister's phone number and address. In the brown notebook, remember? You call me if that grandfather of yours doesn't turn up.' She glared down the track again. 'Or if you need me for anything at all, you hear?'

Ellie nodded and waved, nudging Davey to wave too. 'You've been the best, Mrs Opie. True.'

The old lady reached her seat and leaned forward, her face still anxious. 'I don't know …' she began.

'We'll write,' Ellie called quickly, 'and don't worry, we'll be fine.'

The doors hissed shut, the engine vroomed and the bus chugged forward.

Ellie watched the cloud of white dust disappear towards the main road. The bus was the last link with their old life. She felt a moment of panic as it reached the turn-off. Then it was gone. Her stomach churned over for the tenth time. What now?

Davey gripped her hand tightly. 'I'm going to drive a bus one day.' When Ellie didn't respond, he tugged at her hand and insisted, 'I'll drive one just like Mrs Opie's bus. I'll be the best bus driver in the whole world, I bet.'

'Sure you will, Davey.' Ellie would have agreed to anything just then.

Ms Tori stuck her head out the door. 'You can come inside where it's cool, if you wish. Your grandfather won't be long.'

Ellie smiled carefully. 'Thank you,' she murmured. 'But we're not really hot. We'll be okay here.' And she led her brother to a bench on the verandah.

Davey dragged on her hand, head down, muttering, 'What if he doesn't, Ellie? What if Grandpa doesn't come?'

She faked a casual reply. 'You heard what the lady said, Davey. Grandpa's held up, that's all.'

He was silent for a moment, then, in a small voice, 'You sure Grandpa wants us?'

'Sure he does.' Ellie spoke firmly to convince herself as much as Davey. 'You saw. He wrote in the letter. He's Mum's dad, and our family.'

Davey wasn't convinced. 'I want Mum,' he whispered, tears in his voice.

Ellie swallowed hard. She couldn't trust herself to speak right away. She wanted Mum too. Every bit of her wanted to cry with Davey. To shout and stamp at God to give Mum back. Instead she pulled his small, bony body close.

'Mum's gone, Davey.' She swallowed again and forced her voice to keep steady. 'You know that. Grandpa's all we've got. We're going to live with him now.'

More silence. Then, 'I don't want to live with Grandpa, Ellie. I don't know him. What does he look like?'

She closed her eyes, forcing back the tears. 'I've told you.'

'Tell me again.'

'He's very tall and strong, and Mum loved him very much.' She tried to picture him. 'Mum had a photo, remember? From when she was a kid. In the old album. She was standing next to the laughing man with the big fish. You always asked about him.'

'That one's Grandpa?'

'That one.'

Davey swung his legs back and forwards on the seat. 'Will he take me fishing?'

'Probably. If you don't talk all the time.'

'Does he really look like the picture?'

Ellie had been wondering the same thing. She'd taken the photo out of the album and put it in her private box, along with her diary, the strange drawing and the picture of Mum with that boy. It was there in her bag now. She knew it was old, taken before she was born, but it was proof they had a grandfather.

Her memories of him were hazy. She'd been six when he stayed for a week one Christmas holidays. She hadn't seen him since. That holiday had ended with Mum and Grandpa shouting at each other. Ellie couldn't remember why. Loneliness and fear made her shiver. She didn't want to think or talk just then. But Davey wanted answers. 'Does he Ellie? Does he look like the picture?'

She shoved her hands hard into her jeans pockets. It didn't make any difference whether she remembered him or not. He was their family, their only family, and they were going to live with him forever. It was either that or Family Welfare. Ellie cleared her throat and said loudly, 'Sure. Why not?'

Davey grinned happily. 'He looked nice. I like him.'

'You were just a baby, you couldn't ...' She stopped. She wanted to shout that he couldn't possibly know if he liked Grandpa or not. That Grandpa had fought with Mum over something, and he might be old and cross and not nice at all. But she swallowed her words. Davey would find out soon enough — one way or the other.

Another wave of misery washed through her, making her chest ache. Mum was dead. They would never, never see her again — ever. Nothing would change that, and there was a black pain inside Ellie — a terrible, dark hollow feeling that wouldn't go away.

Davey tugged at her arm. 'Ellie, you're not listening. Where does Grandpa live?'

'He lives in a lighthouse, Davey. I told you — the Larsen's Point lighthouse. Like in the funny drawing. It's along a road out of here, on the top of a cliff by the sea. He looks after the lighthouse and stuff. He's a lighthouse keeper.'

Davey frowned in concentration. 'That'll be our

lighthouse? The one in the drawing? The really high, really round one? Are we going to live in that lighthouse?'

Ellie was struggling with memories. 'I guess so,' she murmured vaguely.

'Will I have a round bedroom — right up high? And a round toilet even higher?'

Ellie shrugged. 'Maybe.' She wasn't sure about anything. Maybe there was a round toilet.

Davey wriggled. 'It'd take a long time to get there — if you were in a hurry.' He was usually in a hurry.

Ellie smiled and hugged her brother again. 'The drawing showed a proper house next to the lighthouse, remember? Most probably we'll live there. And there'll be a proper toilet. There usually is. And we'll be right by the sea.'

Davey swung his legs silently. 'I saw the sea once — when I was five. Mum took us for a holiday, remember? The sea was over the road and the house had a big ginger cat.'

Ellie's mind filled with pictures of Mum splashing, laughing, diving between their legs. 'Mum loved the sea,' she said, and took a deep breath. Her voice husky, she added, 'Now we can go swimming whenever we want. Just like she did. That'll be neat, eh?'

Davey frowned, thinking carefully. 'Swimming's

neat, I guess. Toby Law and Fleck can swim too.'
Toby Law and Fleck were Davey's best mates at
Shelley. 'Toby's making a Lego lighthouse.' The little
boy stared fiercely at the ground, his shoes kicking a
furrow in the dust. After a while he started a small,
private, lighthouse-sea song, all his own.

Ellie closed her eyes, struggling with the
memories. Their lives had changed forever from that
day — that black, worst possible day — the Monday
after her twelfth birthday.

The school principal had called her to his office
and told her. There'd been an accident, he said. Out at
the mine. Some machinery had fallen and crushed
Mum as she walked across the tarmac. She was going
to lunch, and now she was dead. She died in hospital
while Ellie was doing a maths test. The principal had
been very kind. Everyone had been very kind, but
nothing, and no one could bring Mum back …

Tears slid down Ellie's cheeks. She gave in and let
her mind drift back to Shelley, to the company house
at 17 Nugget Street, and the life that had been then.

Shelley was a dot on the map, a green island
surrounded by red earth, spinifex and endless hot
horizons. Water was pumped from under the ground
so they could have grass and trees in town.

According to Mrs Caddy, millions of years ago

there'd been a real sea where the desert was now. They'd gone in the school bus to the edge of the desert and seen layers of shells between red rocks. Ellie had tried to imagine it all sea with waves splashing around the edge.

She remembered a vague mix of places before Shelley. But it was Shelley that meant home to her. They'd moved there when Ellie was six. Davey was just a baby. Dad had taken off and Mum had to get a job. She was secretary out at the mine, and a good one too. The Company had given them a proper house, not just quarters like some of the other ladies. Mum was really respected. Everyone liked her.

Ellie remembered the excitement when they'd heard about the house. Mum had been all flushed and she'd laughed a lot. 'It's no posh mansion,' she'd said. 'But it's private and it's got three bedrooms and a sleep-out out the back. It'll do us.'

And it had. They'd been happy there. Mum made it bright and pretty inside. Ellie had chosen the blue, flowery curtains for her bedroom and the lovely golden ones for the sitting room. They'd painted the kitchen white and blue, and done their best with the shabby porch and the hard gravelly space called a garden.

School had been okay too. There'd been the pool

in Finley Street where everyone went on hot days, and nights too, in the long summer holidays. Then there'd been the Mighty Shelley's Netball Team. She'd been centre — and good at it too. They'd probably have won the cup this year. Well, that's what coach Mr Wally had said. Ellie sighed. What were Anna, Tracy, and the rest of the gang doing right now? Would she ever see them again? Trace'd promised to write but ...

There'd be a school here somewhere. She and Davey would have to go. There'd be new people, explanations, having to start all over again. Ellie swallowed, staring blindly at a spot on the Tourist Centre wall, aching for the life she'd known.

Two months now, it'd been — since Mum was killed.
Ellie had cried inside every single day.

At first, they'd stayed with Mr Wiley, the principal
and his wife. Then Mrs Opie from next door, who
was fat and kind (and who, in their other life, had
driven Mum crazy), had offered to care for the 'poor
motherless mites', until 'other arrangements' could
be made.

To Ellie it hadn't seemed to matter where they
went. Each day was a misery. Davey clinging to her,
demanding she get Mum back, sobbing himself to
sleep every night. She was too numb to cry out loud.

Mrs Opie had done her best, guarding them
through the horror of the funeral and the grim days
afterwards. She'd hugged them hard and done their
washing and meals, and smothered them with

porridge, pink towels and chocolate cake until Ellie had wanted to scream. But at least they were near home and surrounded by the places and faces they knew.

Then Family Welfare had come.

The lady was thin and wore glasses. She had said how 'very concerned for them' she was. And 'how important it was to get back into a routine.' Then she had smiled her anxious businesslike smile and Ellie had wanted to grab Davey and run far out into the desert.

'No other family in the district?' Welfare had asked. 'No Father?'

There had been piles of papers for someone to sign, and hours and hours of 'counselling'. Ellie had hated all the questions, the strangers butting into her life. Mum would have hated it too.

'The Company must pay all expenses. There seems no problem there. Now, what about the father?' Welfare had kept asking and asking. 'We must get in touch with the father.'

Finally Mrs Opie had puffed out her cheeks and her chest. 'No father,' she'd said firmly and took Ms Welfare aside.

Ellie wasn't meant to hear, but she had. 'The man's a weasel,' Mrs Opie had hissed, very red in the face.

'He doesn't want them. He didn't then. He won't now. He disappeared just after young Davey was born. No sight or sound of him since. He could be dead for all they'd know. No loss either.' Then she'd sniffed. Afterwards she'd come and hugged Davey and Ellie tight.

'Nevertheless,' Welfare was very persistent, 'we must do our best to trace the father. And then, if there are no other relatives, they become wards of the state.'

'Over my dead body,' Mrs Opie had snorted. 'They can live with me.'

'It takes time to get proper authorisation,' Ms Welfare had looked over the top of her glasses, and repeated, 'meanwhile the children become wards of the state.'

That was when Ellie had told them about Grandpa.

Welfare had coughed and shaken her head. 'We have no records of grandparents.'

'Well, he's there,' Ellie had almost shouted. 'He's called Hamish McCleod and he's the keeper at Larsen's Point lighthouse. He's our mum's dad. I've got his picture. I've got a drawing of his house.'

Eventually someone had traced him. He had written back immediately. 'They're to come to me,' the letter said. 'Send my grandchildren to me.'

Mrs Opie had shown Ellie the letter. It meant they had someone of their own who wanted them. Strangers weren't going to keep them and tell them what to do. Ellie had asked for a copy and folded it carefully away in her special box with the drawing and the picture of Mum and the boy.

But Welfare was still doubtful. 'We shall have to interview him,' she'd said. 'He's an old man on his own, not our preferred arrangement. Perhaps you'd be better off with us. He lives so far away, Larsen's Point is very remote. Then there's schooling. We'll have to check about schooling ...' There had been other objections.

But Ellie had gritted her teeth and refused to listen. 'He's our grandfather,' she'd said. 'Mum's dad. He wants us.' Mrs Opie had supported her. So had Mrs Wiley and the principal.

Someone went down and interviewed Hamish McCleod. Reluctantly Welfare had agreed that the children could go to him. But on a trial basis only. After a year there'd be a review.

So it had all been arranged. They would go in the school holidays to give them time to adjust. The week after Christmas, Mrs Opie would visit her sister. She would take Ellie and Davey to their grandfather at Larsen's Point at the same time. If things worked out, they'd go to school there.

Now they were here and their grandfather wasn't. The tears dried on Ellie's cheeks and she couldn't think any more.

4

'There you are,' said a voice.

Ellie looked up. A tall, dark shadow was standing between her and the sun. 'Grandpa?' she whispered.

'Ellie,' he said, and crouched down, but didn't touch her. 'A tree fell across the road. I had to wait until they cleared it.' He peered at her and growled, 'You both all right?'

'The lady told us. We're fine.' She glanced up at him shyly. He was nearly as she remembered him. Older than the photo, but the same too. He had crinkly blue eyes and a brown craggy face. His hair was speckled white and faded yellow, like beach sand. She'd have liked to look some more, but she didn't want to be rude.

'Grandpa!' A small body hurtled between them, almost knocking the man to the ground. 'Grandpa!

You came. Will you take us fishing, will you?'

'Davey!' hissed Ellie.

Davey pushed himself to his feet. 'I'm Davey,' he said.

Grandfather stood. 'I know that, son. I came to your first birthday party.'

Davey regarded him solemnly. 'I growed,' — then added in a wobbly voice, 'And now our mum's dead.'

'I know that, too.' The man put his hand on the boy's head. 'That can't be changed, laddie. But you're my family and I'm yours. We should be together now.'

Davey stared up at him. After a moment he nodded. 'Okay,' he said. 'And you can take us fishing.'

Ellie looked away. It was all right for Davey. Everybody loved Davey. Besides he was a boy and Grandpa probably knew about boys. But would he want a girl? Would he want Ellie? She swallowed and glanced quickly at the old man. He had a temper, she knew that. She tried again to remember why Grandpa and Mum had got so mad at each other. He seemed okay now. At least he didn't hug all the time like Mrs Opie.

'It's good that you're here,' he growled, glaring

out from bushy brows. 'I thought those damn Welfare people would never let you go.'

'We're on trial,' murmured Ellie.

'I know!' Grandpa sounded disgusted. 'Damn idiots! As though you'd go anywhere else.'

Davey struck the same pose. 'Yeah,' he copied. 'Damn idiots! We're going to sleep in your house now, aren't we Grandpa?'

Some of the lost feeling dropped away from Ellie. The old man might look fierce and sound like a gravel mixer, but he wasn't going to let anyone else take them.

She saw him turn his face quickly away from Davey and she wondered if he might be smiling. Then he glanced at her. 'I've been getting your rooms ready,' he said. 'Painting. You can choose the curtains.'

'I had blue curtains at home.'

'Blue it is then. We can order from the catalogue. Not pink? I thought all girls liked pink.'

'Ellie hates pink,' said Davey helpfully. 'Mrs Opie likes pink.'

'How about red?'

'I like red,' said Davey.

Grandpa cleared his throat. 'Well, I'm glad someone likes red. We've got lots of red. It stands out against the sea.' He scratched his head. 'I hate pink too, and you can paint your rooms any damn colour you like, so long as it isn't pink.'

Ellie smiled shyly. She sensed he wanted to say something else, but they all stood around in silence. Suddenly Grandpa squatted down, took her hand then Davey's. 'Look, I know you must be very sad about your mum. I'm sad too. We didn't always agree — on a lot of things — but I reckon this is where she'd have wanted you to be. Here at Larsen's Point where she grew up.' He stood without smiling. 'I think Larsen's Point is a good place to live. I hope you will too.' Then he grabbed a duffle bag in each hand and slung them into the back of the big four-wheel drive ute.

Davey came and held Ellie's hand. 'I like Grandpa,' he whispered. 'Don't you?'

Ellie was struggling with the thought of Mum growing up in this place — of being twelve, and living with Grandpa and going to school here and everything.

When she was little, Mum had talked about Larsen's Point all the time. But that was ages ago and Ellie could hardly remember. It had seemed like a magic land, at the other end of Australia. Then Mum and Grandpa had got mad at each other, and Mum had stopped telling them about this place altogether.

But she had kept things, like the faded picture of herself and Grandpa with the fish, and the other one with the boy.

Ellie had taken both photos out of the old album. She wondered who the boy was. Now Mum could never tell her. She swallowed back tears. There were lots of things Mum could never tell them about any more — like the picture of the lighthouse.

Ellie had found it folded into an envelope at the back of the album. The outline had been carefully drawn with different coloured inks on thick, transparent paper like they used in art class. The view was back across a bay and a headland, to the lighthouse tower. There were a lot of wavy lines and spots marked with numbers and names. One said, 'Larsen's Cave?' Or something like that. Maybe the whole thing was a sort of map. Writing on the back asked, *'What do you think Mags? M.'* No name, just 'M'. Ellie wondered who 'M' was. Had 'M' done the drawing? Was he the boy in the photo with Mum? None of it meant anything to her. She'd kept it because it obviously meant something to Mum.

Ellie watched the old man speak to Ms Tori. He could probably tell her who 'M' was — if he chose. There were so many things about Mum he could probably tell her, but would he? Would he want to keep the argument a secret? Would she have to be careful of him for Mum's sake? She even felt vaguely disloyal, just being here, but they had nowhere else to go. Mum's love of the sea came from Larsen's Point, and in her heart, Ellie agreed that Mum would have wanted them to come here — not go to Welfare.

Well, now they *were* here ... and Mum wasn't. The black feeling in Ellie's chest swept over her again. Davey, sensing something, burrowed his head into her tummy. She put her arm round his small body and scuffed the dirt. He tugged on her hand. 'You didn't hear me again, Ellie. I said I like Grandpa, don't you?'

Ellie swallowed. 'I guess so.' She wasn't ready yet to make up her mind. He was okay, so far. He didn't fuss and he didn't expect them to be cheerful and talk all the time like the kids you see on telly. She didn't know why but she felt connected to him. But she couldn't forget that fight with Mum.

He came back and unlocked the side door of the ute. They crowded into the front seat. 'I've got to pick up some supplies from the store,' he said. 'We'd better get going.'

On their way out of town they stopped at Larsen's General Store. The name was written in big red letters on the tin roof. 'Why's the name on the roof?' asked Davey.

Grandpa glanced at Davey from under his brows. 'Why why why, eh Davey?' He backed into the shade then added, 'Olaf Larsen says it's so folk in the big airliners, going to Paris and London, can look down and say, 'Ahh see! There's Larsen's General Store! That must be Larsen's Point!'

'Oh,' breathed Davey and scanned the blue sky for an aeroplane. Ellie thought Grandpa was trying to make a sort of joke, but she didn't say anything.

Inside, the store was dark with a strange mix of smells. The wooden floor wobbled up and down as you walked on it. There was a wide timber counter in front of lots of shelves lined with all sorts of groceries. The rest of the shop was crowded with brooms, mops, shovels, buckets, jacks, hoes, baskets of fishing tackle, a variety of oars and a mess of everything else under the sun. A glass cabinet in one corner held a frilly pink-flowered dinner set, a crystal vase, a green necklace and some white lace doilies.

Ellie knew they were called doilies because once Mum had gone to night school to learn embroidery. She'd only ever made one doily, and Ellie was glad she'd brought it with her. Doilies must be valuable if they keep them in glass cases.

Olaf Larsen stood behind the counter in a blue canvas apron and rumbled at them in a deep voice.

He was a big, bald man with blue eyes and a forked beard, waxed at the end of each side. He shook hands solemnly with Ellie and Davey and told them he was a much better fisherman than their grandfather. Grandpa and he put together a box of groceries and two big tins of bright blue paint. All the while they growled and insulted each other. It was part of an act, Ellie realized; they weren't really mad at each other.

Grandpa signed a slip and picked up the box. 'That's the lot then,' he muttered. 'We're off. Can't stay here yakking all day like some people.'

'Yaa, yaa,' shouted Mr Larsen happily, 'some of us only pretend to vork.' He walked out with them and swung Davey into the front seat of the ute. 'Vun day ve take you fishing, little fella,' he promised. 'Maybe you be better than your grandpappy.'

As they drove out on to the track, the little boy munched contentedly on a chocolate bar. 'I like Mr Larsen,' he beamed. 'And I like his beard. Can I grow one like that, Grandpa?'

Hamish McCleod smothered an oath. 'Put it off a while, eh lad.'

'Is Larsen's Point named after Mr Larsen, Grandpa?' Ellie asked.

'Questions, questions. I'd forgotten about all the questions.' He changed gears and Ellie looked down at her hands, wishing she hadn't said anything.

She heard Grandpa clear his throat, then he said gruffly, 'Questions are all right, girlie. It's the only way you'll find out things. To answer yours: that old fool shopkeeper would like folks to think this place was named after him. It was already called Larsen's Point when he arrived here twenty-five years ago — but Larsen *is* a Swedish name.' He snorted. 'He'll tell you his Viking ancestors discovered Australia, if he can.'

Ellie had learned from Mrs Caddy that the Dutch had discovered Australia. 'Then who is Larsen's Point named after?'

'Ahh,' he shrugged. 'Not the no-good relations of that big tomfool in there, I promise you that.' He flicked a glance sideways and Ellie thought he was smiling inside. 'Olaf and I go fishing together.'

'And he's going to take me,' said Davey comfortably. A moment later they were bumping down the sandy track out of town.

5

By the time they reached the fallen log, the Road Board men had finished clearing the road and were squatting in the shade with mugs of tea. Grandpa waved, called 'G'day,' and drove on.

They rounded a smooth green hill and the sky filled the whole windscreen — lighter, wider and stretching forever. Beneath it lay the sea. And there, in front of them, on a rocky cliff at the edge of the land, was the lighthouse.

'Wow!' breathed Davey. The big round cylinder soared upwards into the blue sky. Its walls sparkled with whitewash and its doors, railings and windows were painted bright red. 'Wow!' breathed Davey again. 'A real lighthouse for us to sleep in!'

'You don't sleep in a lighthouse, son,' Grandpa pointed to the lee of the cliff. 'There's where we sleep — in Lighthouse Cottage.'

Ellie caught her breath. Nestled away from the wind and storms was a low white house with a red roof. The doors and window frames were red, too. Verandahs stretched round three sides, shuttered against the weather. Pale green lawns spread around the house. A few wind-bent trees leaned inwards, and everywhere Ellie looked was the sea.

The ute came to a stop. 'Here we are then,' said Grandpa. He stared at the house as though seeing it for the first time, and added, 'The inside's the same as the outside. Whitewash and red paint. I had a lot of it.'

Ellie squinted against the glare. 'It looks very nice,' she murmured politely.

'Yeah,' said Davey.

A border collie raced barking and bouncing at the side of the ute. Grandpa opened the door and growled, 'Get out of it, Nibs.'

Ellie and Davey climbed down. The dog went on jumping over everybody. 'Down Nibs, here Nibs, jump Nibs!' shouted Davey delightedly. The dog bounced and grinned and gave itself up to a game with the boy, the pair of them rolling and barking and shouting in happy chaos. The old man glared at Nibs, muttering under his breath. But somehow Ellie knew he wasn't really mad.

He led the way across a wide verandah. The front door, painted a bright pillar-box red, opened into a long passage with a skylight above it. Inside, everything sparkled red and white and smelled of paint.

Grandpa pushed open another door. 'This is your room,' he said. Ellie had never had such a big room all to herself. It was lined with white wood from the curved ceiling to the floor. A red iron bed stood in the middle of the room, covered with a white spread. A furry red rug lay beside it. Next to a white corner cupboard stood a red wooden trunk with iron handles. A picture of a sailing ship hung on one wall near a fireplace. The low window looked onto a small garden; the french doors opened onto the verandah.

Grandpa cleared his throat. 'As I said, lots of red and white.' He looked at Ellie and frowned. 'We've got the blue paint now. And you can pick out some curtains and a bedspread.'

Ellie smiled shyly. Grandpa had made it nice for her. He wouldn't have done that if he didn't want them. A little bit of the black feeling inside her fell away. 'It's like the inside of a ship,' she said. 'I saw one on telly once. Maybe blue curtains'd be neat, but ... ummm, red's neat too.'

Davey had a smaller room next door. 'Can I sleep here?' he said. 'With Ellie?'

The old man scratched his nose. 'It's up to you and Ellie,' he said. 'Now you'd better come and have a sandwich.'

The kitchen was huge and white with an ancient wood
stove and a big pine table in the middle of the room.
The windows opened outwards and below each one
was a window seat, carved into the wall. Sunlight
streamed through another skylight, cut into the roof.

'I've never seen windows in the roof before,' said
Davey. 'You'd have to be taller than you Grandpa to
see out of them.'

The old man looked up. 'They're to let in the day.
These old houses are dark so I put sun holes in.
They're called skylights.'

'They're nice,' Davey stared up thoughtfully.
'They'd be moon holes and star holes too,' he said.

Ellie loved the whole room. It was even more like
being on board a ship.

'Lunch,' growled Grandpa and took thick

sandwiches and a carton of chocmilk out of a bumpy old refrigerator.

They sat at the pine table and munched sausage and lettuce sandwiches. 'I love sausage sandwiches,' mused Davey, swinging his legs back and forward. 'And chocmilk, and hamburgers, and crumbed chicken, and ice-cream and custard tart and …'

'I don't know about custard tart,' said the old man. 'I'm not fancy.' He nodded at a small electric griller on the bench. 'I cook on that, mostly.' After a while he added, 'Sometimes I light the wood stove in winter.'

'Ellie can cook,' announced Davey.

'Davey!' Ellie frowned across the table.

'She made me a birthday cake once.' He ignored her and then added generously, 'She'll make you one, too.'

'Thank you,' said Grandpa solemnly, not looking at Ellie. He stood up. 'I'll show you the beach. You can explore the rest of the house in your own time.'

'The toilet?' asked Davey quickly.

'Out there, next to the wash-house.' Davey disappeared and Ellie rinsed the dishes at the sink. Grandpa dried.

Davey returned. 'It's not round!' he hissed at Ellie. 'But it's huge — with a chain!' Ellie was sure she saw Grandpa hide a smile.

They went through a brick courtyard and down a grassy bank towards the sea. In the curve of the cliff was a sheltered cove with a small white beach and smooth blue-green water.

'Ohhhh,' murmured Ellie. 'It's so beautiful.' She looked up suddenly, her memory jogged. 'Is this ...'

'Our Beach.' Grandpa finished for her. 'It was one of your mother's favourite places.' He squinted against the sun. 'Sometimes she shared it with me. That's why she called it Our Beach.'

'I remember now,' whispered Ellie. 'She told me about it once.'

Grandpa looked away frowning. Ellie thought he wished they hadn't spoken about Mum. She wished so too.

'I swim here most mornings,' he said, eyeing them sternly. 'Can you both swim?'

Davey sat down, pulling at his shoelaces. 'I can do dead-man's float and dog paddle. You watch me.'

'Show me tomorrow, son,' said Grandpa.

'We both had classes in the Finley Street Pool at Shelley,' Ellie added. 'I passed my Intermediate. Davey passed the Floaters.'

The old man squatted down. 'Okay then ... We need a few basic rules here. I can't be with you all day, so you have to be sensible. First off, most of the time, Our Beach is calm, shallow and very safe. Except in a forty knot gale. You can play down here as long as you tell me first, okay?' Ellie and Davey nodded.

'The rest of the coast is all right in most places, most times. But there are some dangerous spots. You go nowhere without discussing it with me first. Okay?' The children nodded again.

'And you Davey, are not to go in the water at any time without either Ellie, me or an older person. All right?'

Davey screwed up his nose. 'Is this forever?'

'Or until you pass your Intermediate.'

Davey sighed heavily.

'These aren't just stupid rules, son,' Grandpa held Davey's arms, and fixed him with his eyes. 'This is to keep you safe. We have to look out for each other. I want you both to promise to keep the rules. They're common sense. Promise?'

Ellie murmured, 'Promise.'

Davey crossed his heart and spat carefully on the sand. 'Cross my heart and hope to die,' he whispered solemnly.

Grandpa looked at them both for a long time. Then he almost grinned. 'Okay.' He crossed his heart and spat, too. 'Okay. And I'll promise to look after you the best I can.' He thrust out his hand. 'Deal?'

Ellie and Davey put their hands on top of Grandpa's. 'Deal,' they said together.

7

The next day, Grandpa said it was time to check the lighthouse. 'Not that it needs a man to run it any more,' he growled. 'It's all done by computers and radio beacons now.' It sounded like a sort of sigh to Ellie. He reached for the key and they went outside and stared at the stark white tower with its red railings and red door.

'You know,' he rumbled. 'They can see her almost forty kilometres out to sea.' Ellie could hear the pride in his voice. 'She's a link between ship and shore,' he went on, 'flashing her signal night after night so ships can navigate by her. It's what it's all about — a lifeline to those at sea.' Then he went a bit red in the face and added, 'Only the small ships need us nowadays.'

'Why do you call the lighthouse she, Grandpa?'

asked Davey. 'Do they have boy lighthouses, too?'

The old man snorted. 'As far as I know they're all females, son. Like ships too … difficult, fussy, hard work, but occasionally worth it.'

Davey hooted, not quite sure of his meaning, but enjoying the man-to-man feel of it. He pulled a face at Ellie and she pulled one back.

They crossed the green lawn to the tower. The sea breeze was in and clouds tossed around the sky. In the cove, the sea was choppy with small wavelets creaming onto the beach. Nibs bounced and squirmed round Davey's legs, begging for a walk or a play.

'Scoot dog,' muttered the old man as he bent to check the readings on the weather equipment, speaking details into his mobile recorder. 'Looks fine for a while,' he said.

The old brass key to the main door was about the size of Ellie's hand. It slid into the well-oiled lock and turned without a hitch. Right in front of them a scrolled iron staircase spiralled upwards. They began to climb, feet clattering on the red metal steps.

In the main lamp room, the polished brass fittings and prisms were almost blinding. 'Keep going right on up,' said the old man. 'You can go outside too, if you're careful. And young Davey,' he held his shoulder, 'no climbing the railings.'

Up and up they went, Davey bounding like a young pup, stopping every now and then to catch his breath. Ellie wasn't far behind. Passing the first landing, they raced to the top. Ellie slid the bolt to the balcony and they pushed outside. The wind hit them with a wallop. Sky and clouds whirled around in a dizzy kaleidoscope of movement. Ellie found it hard to stop her head spinning. Wind howled into her eyes and whipped at her hair. Davey pretended to stagger like a drunk, rolling round and round the walkway until Ellie became scared he'd topple over.

Far out to sea was a ship. She imagined the captain at his helm, watching the lighthouse through his telescope, wondering who the two strange figures were. She waved just in case.

On the land side, scrub hid the track leading to Larsen's Point township. The coastline stretched out both ways in a myriad of small bays and cliffs. Everywhere was the sea, white-capped against deep blue, the spray blowing back into the circling gulls. Ellie felt like a gull herself, free and spiralling into the wind. For the first time in two months and thirteen days, she forgot the pain of her mother's death.

After a while, she hauled Davey inside and they staggered back down to Grandpa. He was marking something on a chart.

'Whooommm!' shouted Davey, still in a whirl with the wind. 'Whooooom, whoooom!' He rolled his eyes and charged round the room, waving his arms like a lunatic. 'Take-off! Phrooooom. Prepare for landing! Phroooooom.'

'Lunch,' announced Grandpa.

Later they sat munching more sausage and lettuce sandwiches. Davey swallowed and said seriously, 'I'm going to be a lighthouse keeper when I grow up, Grandpa. I'll help you look after Larsen's Point,' he grinned and stuck out his tongue at Ellie. 'Even if *she's* a lot of trouble.'

The old man shrugged and pushed his plate away. 'Too late, son. Lighthouse keepers are a thing of the past. Like I said, it's all done by computer gizmos nowadays.'

'But you're a lighthouse keeper, Grandpa,' said Ellie. 'The bus driver said so.'

He snorted his amusement. 'Well, I must be then, mustn't I!' He shook his head. 'Yeah well, Bill Dunbar knew me when I was the official keeper. When radio beacons came in, they didn't need a lighthouse or its keeper any more. There's a sign outside says RANGER and that's what I am these days — Ranger, official weather man, environmental officer, heritage guardian and general dogsbody.'

'Okay,' said Davey cheerfully. 'I'll be those too.'

His grandfather gave a dry laugh. 'You do that lad. At least we can all live right here.'

'Of course,' said Davey. He'd never imagined otherwise. 'Then there'll be you and me and Ellie and Nibs — forever. And sometimes Mr Larsen.'

'And sometimes Mr Larsen,' repeated Grandpa with a wry grin.

In her wildest dreams, Ellie couldn't imagine that anyone would be lucky enough to own Lighthouse Cottage. She couldn't help asking, 'Will we really be able to stay here forever, Grandpa?'

He glanced at her and nodded. 'Back then, no one wanted to look after a house more than a hundred and fifty years old, so I bought it.' He grunted and added, 'Good thing too. It counted with Welfare — owning a house.'

Ellie felt warm inside. Lighthouse Cottage belonged to Grandpa. No one could take it away from them. She stared round the old, not quite-octagonal kitchen. Every odd-shaped cupboard gave her new pleasure.

Early that morning she and Davey had explored the whole rambling building. Even after so short a time, she felt comforted by it. Strange and old-fashioned it might be, but the rooms fitted together in a well-used sort of way. Now it would be their home forever.

Grandpa had said the house was at least a hundred and fifty years old. All sorts of winter storms and summer heatwaves must have beaten against its sloping roof and sturdy walls. Ellie reckoned it would still be the same two hundred years from now. Most important of all, it was specially connected to her because Mum had grown up here. Mum had swum and played in the cove of Our Beach. She'd slept in the same wood-lined room, even in the very bed that was Ellie's now. The smell of dried grass and salt and seaweed were the same smells Mum knew. Now she and Davey would know those things too.

Ellie had to admit to herself that their modern bungalow in Shelley was nothing like this. There wouldn't be another home like Lighthouse Cottage in the world! Everything about it seemed so right, even the trapdoor in her bedroom ceiling! Beyond it must lie an attic. Not that she'd ever seen an attic.

As for the bathroom — it was something else! Stuck on to one end of the verandah, with a huge old tub with red-painted lion's feet, big brass taps, no shower and a gas water-heater that boomed like a bomb every time you lit it.

The laundry (or what Grandpa called the wash-house) was down the brick path, near the vegetable garden. The walls and roof of the toilet next to it were covered in a pink-flowering creeper. Mum would have said it was fit for a duchess. The toilet itself was huge, with a red-painted seat, a pile of *Australian Geographic* magazines on the floor and a dangling chain that Ellie found hard to work. Further past the vegetable garden Grandpa's chooks perched on a huge old wagon, almost white from bird droppings.

And in the background, around, behind and in front of everything was the sea. Ellie could hear it, smell it and see it. This morning, in the wind round the lighthouse, she had even tasted it.

Lying in bed the night before, she had listened to the rising tide and the suck and woosh of the waves. In some ways it was like the wind blowing in from the red desert at Shelley. Always there, changing but unchanged. The old house by the sea would be there forever too.

Grandpa must have read her mind. 'Lighthouse Cottage has been here a long time,' he said. 'It's got secrets.'

Ellie and Davey sat forward. 'Secrets?' whispered Davey.

'Every room has its secrets, laddie.' The old man poured himself a cup of tea.

Ellie's eyes widened. 'The door in my bedroom ceiling? And the funny cupboard?'

Grandpa glanced sideways at Ellie. 'Your mother told you, huh?'

Ellie flushed. 'I knew Mum grew up here ... with you. That's about all.' She took a deep breath. 'She ... that is, she didn't ...'

'Didn't tell you much about me or the old place, eh?' Grandpa's voice sounded sharp, almost rough. 'I expected as much.' He looked as if he were about to say something else, then shook his head. 'Well, it doesn't matter now. C'mon then.'

Ellie found she'd been holding her breath. He'd been going to say something about Mum, something about why she'd never told them things, then he'd changed his mind. She wasn't sure whether she wished he'd gone on, or not. Anyway the moment had passed, Davey was racing off down the hall.

8

Ellie's bedroom cupboard had a bend in it. She could walk right in to hang up her clothes. But at the end it turned a corner, and went deeper into the wall. She'd put her private box there on a shelf right at the back. Grandpa pushed aside her clothes and reached behind the shelf. 'There's a catch here somewhere,' he grunted. All of a sudden there was a click, and a panel at the back swung open.

'Wow!' gasped Davey and rushed into the dark space beyond. 'Neat!'

Ellie wandered through, her mouth gaping, her voice an unbelieving squeak. 'A secret room! That's epic, Grandpa! Amazing!'

He gave a half-smile. 'Mags … your mother, called it a pirate hole.'

'Pirates?' whispered Davey, round-eyed. 'Was it? Is it?'

The old man shrugged. 'Well, who knows? On the other hand, it might have been a passageway that was made into a wardrobe when they put the timber lining in.'

Davey was certain it was for pirates, possibly even aliens. He crawled back and forwards, round and through, and thought he might put his bed in there.

'Then we'd never get to use the secret tunnel,' objected Ellie.

'Okay,' he agreed. There was no further mention of sleeping in Ellie's room.

Behind a pile of boxes in the pantry was a trapdoor with a wooden ramp leading to an underground room. It was the size of Mrs Opie's double garage. Grandpa switched on the torch and beamed its light round the room. 'The cellar,' he said.

Davey rushed ahead clattering down the ramp to the stone floor, enjoying the echo. Ellie walked slowly, fingers trailing on walls of solid rock. 'Wow! This is incredible.' Then she shivered. 'But it's so cold.'

'It's a cold store,' said Grandpa, flashing the torch at rows of wooden shelves, some filled with boxes of what looked like tomatoes and some other produce. 'Before fridges everything was stored down here — butter, meat, milk, fresh vegetables — all the preserves and supplies. Works pretty well too, keeps things fresh, and it's too cold for most bugs and rats.'

'Rats? There are rats?' Ellie gulped.

'Oh, there are always rats.' Grandpa seemed to hide a smile. 'Everywhere. Even Shelley.'

Davey attacked imaginary rats with an imaginary gun. 'Booom, booom raatattttaaatt!' Echoes thundered round the store.

Grandpa winced. 'In the old days, after a shipwreck, the keepers might've had to feed forty or fifty people. I still store vegetables in here and my ginger beer in the summer. It makes a good wine cellar, too.' He nodded upwards. 'There's one more place you should know about.'

Jutting against the outside wall of the kitchen was a knee-high limestone lean-to. On top of it was another hatch. This one was stiff and heavy to shift. The hinges creaked as the old man heaved at it. 'I keep cleaning materials for the lighthouse down here. They can be pretty strong stuff so don't touch them. And I don't want you kids in here on your own.' He shone his torch on a ladder leading downwards. 'These steps could be slippery.'

Davey clambered down like a monkey. Ellie followed slowly, trying not to think about rats. It was like climbing into a dark hole and she was glad of Grandpa and his torch. The beam picked out another cellar, even colder and darker than the first. It smelled of kerosene, rope and the sea. She was aware of a faint boom vibrating through the floor.

'Is that the sea? Is this a cave or something?' she asked.

Her grandfather nodded. 'One of many. The whole coastline is honey-combed with a network of caves. During a good storm you'll feel the echo of waves in the house.'

Ellie shivered. She imagined lying in bed at night with the feel of the storm rising through the floor. It was both exciting and scary.

Davey scuttled over to wriggle in between Ellie and Grandpa. 'It's a dungeon,' he whispered. 'A real dungeon. I don't like it. People got chained up down here.' He threw a worried look at Grandpa.

The old man flashed his torch onto a pair of iron rings bolted to the stone wall. 'That's possible,' he said. Ellie thought she heard a smile in his voice. 'But those rings are more for tying up ropes.'

'Not pirates or anything?' Davey sounded almost disappointed.

'Well, of course for pirates, if any turn up,' growled Grandpa. 'There haven't been any lately. In the 1860s, one of the keepers kept a couple of Irish convicts hidden down here for a few weeks. But mostly it's just a place to store rope and emergency equipment.'

Ellie was trying to picture the two desperate men, huddled in the darkness, listening to the boom and thump of the waves and wondering what their fate might be. 'What happened to the convicts?'

Grandpa scratched his nose. 'Well, according to local legend they escaped on an American whaling ship for Boston. The police accused Keeper O'Grady — who was also Irish — of giving them a hand, but they couldn't prove anything. The men were due to hang.'

Davey made pretend strangling noises. 'Why were they going to be hanged, Grandpa?'

The old man flicked the torch round the cellar. 'For mutiny — something like that. Time to go, I think.'

Ellie had wandered over to examine the bolts in the wall. There seemed to be a pattern of scratching below the rings. She crouched down. 'Grandpa there's some marks or something here.'

'Yes,' he said. He didn't sound particularly excited, but he held the torch steady for her.

She peered closely, hands running over the rough edges of the rock. 'It says,' she squinted, '*O.S.L. 1756.*' She looked up startled. '1756! Grandpa what … is it a date?'

He shrugged and scowled. 'Maybe, maybe not.'

'But if it is a date, who could have done it? No one was supposed to be here then — no Europeans anyhow.'

He shrugged again. 'So we've been told.'

Ellie knew 1756 was long before European settlement. There weren't supposed to be any settlers, any soldiers or, as far as she knew, even explorers around here in 1756, only Aborigines, and they wouldn't have scratched a date. The wall was hardened limestone, the letters and numbers well-formed. It would have taken patience and a strong hand on a knife to have carved them into the rock. 'So who carved *O.S.L. 1756*, Grandpa?'

The old man scowled, then gave one of his wry grins. 'Kids, they say.' Ellie looked doubtful and he went on, 'It's a long story, lass. I'll tell you some other time. Right now, let's get out of here.'

Her mind was in a whirl. She had a million questions but Davey was already halfway up the ladder.

'It's awful dark in the dungeon,' he gulped. 'I bet it's haunted.' Then he added loudly, 'I wasn't scared. I bet I wasn't scared!'

'I bet you weren't either, son.'

Ellie saw Grandpa's face soften as he reached out

clumsily to ruffle the little boy's hair. 'It's okay to be
scared sometimes Davey, lad,' he muttered. 'The
hatch got stuck on me once and I was trapped in the
pitch black for nearly four hours. I was scared then, I
can tell you.' He shuddered. 'Nowadays, I keep a
pressure lamp and a few supplies down there.
Neither of you is to go down on your own. Is that
clear?' Davey nodded solemnly. Ellie had no
intention of going down there alone. Davey
wouldn't either.

Outside, Ellie lifted her face to the sun. Shifting
her eyes to the roof, she asked, 'What about an attic,
Grandpa? It looks like there should be an attic.'

'I suppose you can call it that. It's just a huge
space in the roof.' He pointed to a trapdoor on the
roof above his head. 'There used to be rungs up to
that entrance, near the chimney. There's another one
in ...'

'My bedroom,' finished Ellie.

He glanced at her. 'Right. It's painted over. You
can't open it.'

Ellie thought he sounded much fiercer when he
spoke to her. Maybe because she was a girl. She
hung her head and shrugged to show she didn't
really care — but of course she did.

'Can we go up to the attic?' persisted Davey,

trying to pull himself onto a window ledge.

Grandpa grunted, half amused, half impatient. 'Not right now, boy. Give me time to fix the rungs first. There's nothing up there but a lot of possum and bird dirt, plenty of spiders and some old rubbish.'

'Any of Mum's things?' whispered Ellie.

'Unlikely. I gave most of her stuff away.' The old man glanced at his watch and missed the shock on Ellie's face. He went on, 'Anyhow, right now I've got things to do.' And he stomped off towards the lighthouse buildings.

Ellie watched him go, her senses fizzing. Secret hideaways, Irish convicts, *O.S.L. 1756* carved on the dungeon wall — now 'old rubbish' in the attic! No matter what Grandpa said, Ellie was ready to bet Mum would have kept stuff up there. It'd be just the sort of place for special secrets. Excitement shot through her. Well ... There was plenty of time, the rest of the long holidays ahead. One by one she would unfold the secrets of the house.

9

Each day that passed, Ellie grew less and less put off by Grandpa's fierce glare and gruff voice. They never turned into anything worse and she guessed he was often smiling inside. A lot of the time she almost forgot her worries about the fight he had with Mum — but not quite. One day she'd learn the truth about that. Right now she was really keen to know about those marks on the dungeon wall.

A few evenings later, when Davey went off to watch his favourite telly show, she went looking for Grandpa. The sun had dropped behind the point, edging the clouds with strips of gold. The lighthouse stood out tall and dark against the western sky. Grandpa was on the verandah watching, as he did each night, the beam from the big lamp sweep across the sea. But Ellie was in no mood for beams or sunsets. It was the scratchings she wanted to find out about. Knocking her foot against the railing to get his attention, she asked, 'Grandpa what about *O.S.L. 1756*? Is O.S.L. a person? Is 1756 a date? What about it?'

He flicked a glance at her then looked down at his charts. 'I wondered how long before your curiosity got the better of you.' He scratched his nose. 'Don't let your imagination run away with you, lass. It's nothing important.'

Ellie didn't believe him. 'You mean somebody knows, actually knows, for certain sure, it's not important?'

'Something like that.'

'Some expert's checked it out and everything?'

He frowned over his glasses at a detail on his chart and didn't look at her. 'That's right and the important people who know important things say it was either the convicts who built the place or children around the turn of the century.'

'You're kidding.'

'Not at all. The official ruling is that at some time or another, some keeper's kids got into the cellar and scratched graffiti on that wall.'

'Is that what you think, Grandpa?'

'It doesn't matter what I think, lass. As they said,

it's not my business, and that's the official ruling.'

Ellie pulled a disbelieving face. 'It's not the sort of thing kids would go to all that trouble to do. They might scratch some initials or something, but not that much, or that deep. It'd be too hard. Convicts could've, I guess,' she added reluctantly.

Grandpa shrugged. 'Don't ask me. I'm not the expert.'

Ellie wanted to shake him. Make him tell her more. She kicked the rail and stared out to sea. 'Well I don't believe it.'

The old man laughed dryly. 'Suit yourself.' Then he added, 'I go with the convict theory, myself. They all had numbers, you know. 1756 could be a number.' He got his charts together and stood up. 'Anyway, take it from me, it's not worth following up. All the checking's been done already.'

He was almost out the door when Ellie asked, 'By Mum you mean? Did Mum do a lot of checking?'

The old man didn't answer for some time. Then he ground out, 'I knew you were going to ask me that. Yes, your mother did her best to find out more. It was one of the things we disagreed about. She was ready to believe all sorts of theories.'

'Such as?'

'Such as nothing that could be proved! Nothing

that amounted to anything.' He turned and glared at Ellie, muttering, 'I should never have taken you kids down there.' Then he stomped off.

Ellie stayed staring out at the big beam lighting up the sea. He wasn't telling her everything. She just knew it. All that rumbling and carry-on meant he was trying to put her off. Well, she was certain kids hadn't carved those figures. Possibly a convict could have done it, but whoever … if Mum kept looking, then so would she. Besides there had to be some other explanation. There just had to be.

10

The thought of what *O.S.L. 1756* might mean filled
Ellie's mind. Several times she tried to bring up the
subject but each time Grandpa brushed off any
further talk about it. The only new information came
about one day when they were driving into town for
supplies.

Davey, always impressed by Olaf Larsen's beard,
was chattering happily about growing one like it
some day. Then out of the blue he asked, 'Did Mr
Larsen carve those letters in the dungeon?'

Grandpa gave a snort of laughter and said, 'I
wouldn't put it past him, lad. He's mad keen to have
folks believe his ancestors found the place. But, no.
The Larsen name is just a coincidence. There are as
many Larsens in Sweden as there are Smiths in
Australia. Anyway this place was called something

like "Larsen" even before white men came here. Certainly before Olaf Larsen stuck his hairy face in the general store.'

Ellie lifted her head and stared. She saw his jaw clench. He probably didn't mean to say what he'd said, but she followed up quickly with, 'So the 'L' in O.S.L. could stand for Larsen, Grandpa? And that's how the town got its name?'

He changed gears loudly and shot a fierce glance across at her. 'I never said the O.S.L. was anything to do with Larsen. I'm only saying what Olaf Larsen would like us all to think.'

'But you said this place was called Larsen before white men came here. How do you know that?'

'Great balls of fire, girl! Don't you ever let up? You're as bad as your mother.' Ellie stared up at him, saying nothing. After a while he muttered, 'Some of the old blokes — local Aboriginal fellas, reckoned they'd called the place something that sounded like Larsen, long before white men came here.'

Ellie looked down at her hands, her stomach churning with excitement. So Grandpa must've believed there was something strange about the scratchings. He *had* done more checking. He'd checked with local Aborigines. She frowned, running the name over in her mind. 'But Larsen is

Swedish isn't it? Not an Aboriginal word?'

'Of course it's not. Anything, even a crow, can sound like Larsen if you want it to. Just as Olaf Larsen swears his ancestors discovered the place, or some such nonsense, the old blokes round here'll tell you what you want to hear. None of it amounts to anything!' And he skidded the ute to a halt in front of the general store.

'But ...' began Ellie.

'No buts, girl. Now come on. We can't hang around here all day!'

Ellie put her head down. No matter how much puffing and blowing Grandpa went on with, she was certain that he believed the L in O.S.L. meant Larsen.

The mild summer days passed peacefully enough. The sun, the wind-washed sky and long swims in their small sandy cove soothed Ellie, body and soul. She fell into bed each night, slept without remembered dreams and woke to a growing pleasure in each day. She began to feel safe and secure in her little world and wanted nothing more — just the three of them and Nibs at Lighthouse Cottage, forever.

Each day she got to know more of the surrounding bays and countryside. Keeping (mostly) to Grandpa's rules, she and Davey rambled up and down the cliffs and beaches close to Lighthouse Cottage. She had some vague idea of checking for other caves near the house. Maybe there'd be more scratchings — something that'd help her find out what *O.S.L. 1756* meant. But the caves she could get into easily were sea-swept, and bare of any markings.

One entrance was cut deep into a darkness in the cliff side. Rough limestone stalactites and spiders' webs blocked the opening, and there was a rank smell of slime, feral animals and rotting vegetation. She peered hesitantly through the a gap in the rocks. Davey didn't like it either. 'I can't see the lighthouse from down here,' he said uneasily and moved into the sunlight. 'If we go in there we won't see it — even worser. And we promised Grandpa.'

Ellie had no more wish to try the cave than Davey. In the end, she decided to give up cave-hunting for a while, and concentrate on Davey's swimming lessons. He took to the water like a young seal, sliding and diving and romping with Nibs until the sea seemed as natural to him as the land. When Grandpa gave them masks and snorkels they spent hours exploring the inside reef of Our Beach. It was like finding a new world on the doorstep.

Fishing was a different story. Twice they went out in the dinghy with Grandpa and Olaf Larsen. The first time it was a hot, still day. The water was clear and calm below the dinghy and Ellie was happy to lean over the edge and watch schools of fish dart in and out of the drifting weed. Davey caught two herring, a cod and a skippy. He talked about it for days afterwards. He would catch a shark one day, he was going to be a fisherman when he grew up. He couldn't wait for the next time.

A week later they went out again. Ellie didn't think it was all that neat. The fish were biting, but taking the hook out of the fish's mouth was definitely yuk. Grandpa refused to do it for her. 'You've got to learn yourself, lass,' he said. 'If you're going to catch 'em and eat 'em, you have to kill 'em yourself — that's only fair on the fish.'

Ellie wasn't keen on either choice. In the end she gave up and scanned the cliffs for the network of caves that Grandpa had talked about. The view of the coastline from here reminded her of something but she couldn't remember what. She wondered about a darkened area below the cottage but that area was partly under water with waves surging around it, and too hard to see if there were caves there. No one could reach it anyway and Ellie certainly wasn't going to try.

After a while the breeze came in and the water turned choppy. Ellie began to feel queasy. Davey, who seemed to have a cast iron stomach, carefully disembowelled his second herring on the side of the dinghy next to her. Her stomach heaved. She hung over the bow, ready to swim the three kilometres into shore, or drown. Grandpa, rolling his eyes at her pale green face, muttered something under his breath and started the engine for home.

Ellie crouched in the front of the boat, soaked from spray, remembering that picture of Grandpa and Mum with the fish. She sighed and closed her eyes. Mum was probably a real cool sailor. Mum could probably take hooks out of any old fish's mouth. Olaf Larsen leaned forward and wrapped her in his huge warm sweater but Ellie was too miserable to care. She fixed her eyes on the beach, and hung on grimly to what was left of her lunch.

When they reached the shore, she insisted on helping push the dinghy above the high tide line and carting the gear home. Grandpa gave her a thoughtful look, but said nothing. Olaf patted her hair and said gently, 'No worries, girlie, ve manage. It be better next time.' Ellie was determined there wasn't going to be a next time.

She got her appetite back for dinner. The others had fish, but Ellie was quite happy to settle for vegies and a baked potato sprinkled with melted cheese.

'If Ellie can't eat the fish, I can't eat my Brussels sprouts,' announced Davey.

'It's not the same,' Ellie selected a large sprout and

munched on it. 'You just don't like green veggies.'

'Green's the colour of your face in the boat,' Davey beamed at her. 'Brussels Sprout Face!' he shouted, delighted with his own wit.

Ellie rolled her eyes and shrugged. 'Fish face,' she drawled. 'You know what Grandpa said, "If you don't catch 'em, you don't eat 'em." Well, I didn't catch any fish.'

'Well I didn't catch the Brussels sprouts,' Davey poked his tongue at her, still vastly pleased with himself. 'So I don't have to ...'

'Eat, boy!' rumbled Grandpa. 'Every single one of them!'

Davey's bottom lip came out. 'Awrrrr! I don't have to.'

'Yes, you do,' said Grandpa, removing the backbone from his herring. 'Because I say so, and I take you fishing.' They glared at each other. Moments passed, then Davey began eating his sprouts. Looking up, Ellie caught Grandpa's eye. He was smiling inside again. Somehow she knew then, it didn't matter all that much about being seasick and not wanting to kill the fish.

12

As the days passed there were times when Ellie hardly thought of the old life at all. The black lonely ache was still there — it always would be — but it didn't sweep over her as often as it used to, and the pain stayed at a distance, somehow muffled over.

As for Davey, he was the carefree boy he'd once been. He followed Grandpa round like a shadow and confided endless special secrets to Nibs, who was only too happy to share them.

One morning Ellie helped Grandpa store his tomatoes in the cold store. It was almost empty now, but she imagined the shelves full of supplies, and herself coping with a houseful of castaways from a ship, wrecked on those rocks out there.

Of course, the cold store wasn't the dungeon. There was no way she'd go back to the dungeon without Grandpa, and only then to get another look at the scratchings. He was still playing dumb about that. The attic was another slippery topic. Grandpa hadn't got round to mending the ladder and Ellie suspected he was stalling. Mum would have left stuff in the attic. Surely that's why Grandpa didn't want them up there.

The house and all its secrets continued to enchant her and she found surprises in nearly every room. The linen closet opened out into a series of other closets stacked with hand-embroidered tablecloths and masses of doilies. Grandpa certainly never used hand-embroidered tablecloths or doilies. Perhaps a woman from one of the lighthouse families spent hour after lonely hour embroidering them for tea parties that never happened. A desk in the sitting room had a secret compartment that contained a small pearl-covered sewing box. Maybe that lonely woman kept her embroidery cottons in the box. The thought made Ellie sad.

Then she found the old photo album. It was in the bottom of a window seat in a spare bedroom. It had a picture of two dogs on the battered cover and an inscription that read: *This book belongs to Maggie McCleod. Private.*

Ellie sat on the cool wooden floor and slowly

turned the thick green pages. Mum squinted back at her from every angle. Mum in a flower girl's dress, Mum with friends down at the beach, Mum next to a huge sandcastle. There was a special one of Mum, eyes screwed up against the sun, with Grandpa and a seal on the rocks below the lighthouse. And lots with Mum dwarfed against the lighthouse's soaring tower, dress and hair tossed in the wind. There were several of a dog, something like Nibs, and two or three with the same tall, skinny, dark-haired boy who was in Ellie's photo in her special box. There were school photos, with Mum looking much like Ellie did now, all legs and ponytail. And there was a copy of the one of Mum and Grandpa holding a fish.

Ellie reached the last photo and turned back to the beginning again. It brought such a sweet sadness that tears ran down her cheeks onto the page. She went through it five times, focusing on Mum, trying to guess her thoughts and feelings. After lunch she found a spot on the side verandah, out of the wind, and shared the book with Davey.

'Mum!' shouted Davey. 'There's that fish one with Grandpa.' He laughed over the dog like Nibs and asked, 'Who's that boy? Is it Dad?'

'No,' said Ellie shortly, 'just a friend.' She wondered who the boy was too.

'Mum looks like you, Ellie,' announced Davey. And Ellie had to catch her breath. The little boy flicked through the last few photos and back to the one with Grandpa and the fish again. Then he wriggled away, calling Nibs.

Ellie couldn't believe it. She wrinkled her brows and asked, 'Davey, don't you want to look some more?'

'I seen 'em,' he said firmly.

'But these were of Mum when she lived here.' Ellie tried not to sound shocked at his casual treatment of her discovery.

Davey frowned. 'She's not here now.' Then he jumped off the verandah and disappeared around the side of the house, leaving Ellie feeling angry and let down. Davey didn't seem to miss Mum like he used to.

But Davey brought it up again at dinner that evening. 'Ellie's got a book of pictures of Mum,' he announced to Grandpa. 'She's keeping it.'

'Davey!' hissed Ellie. She hadn't wanted to tell Grandpa — hadn't known what he'd say.

The old man put down his knife and fork and stared at Ellie. 'Oh yes?'

'It was in a window seat,' she glared at her grandfather. 'On the front it says "This book belongs to Maggie McCleod. Private." I guess it belongs to me now. Davey doesn't want it.'

Grandpa started eating again. 'I guess it does. No problem with that.'

'You said you gave everything away.' Ellie's cheeks were pink. She meant to sound mad, but to her own ears it sounded like whingeing.

There was a long silence.

Finally Grandpa spoke. 'You got something on your chest, lass? Something you want to talk about?'

Davey slid off his chair to curl up with Nibs under the table.

Ellie's heart was beating fast and she tried to stop her voice sounding squeaky. 'I want to talk about Mum.'

The old man nodded slowly. 'Go ahead then. Nothing's stopping you.'

The heat went out of Ellie. She felt kind of flat, but she pushed on. 'You and Mum got real mad at each other,' she mumbled.

'That's right. We truly did. I regret it. So did she, probably. What did she tell you?'

Ellie sank into her chair. 'She didn't tell us hardly anything. Nothing about this house, or her friends, or her dog … just nothing.' The hurt was so bad she couldn't find the right words.

There was another long silence. After a while the old man nodded. 'I guessed that. When they didn't let me know about the accident right away. When I didn't hear from you.' He shook his head. 'We've got a damn stubborn streak in this family, and Mags and I are probably the worst.' He stared straight at Ellie. 'Well we've got to talk about her sometime. It might as well be now.'

Ellie took a shaky breath. She was unsure whether she could handle this or not. But she had asked for it. She wanted to know what happened between Mum and Grandpa.

Grandpa frowned. 'You remember that time I came to stay?'

Ellie nodded and stared hard at her hands clenched tightly in her lap. 'Davey's first birthday. That was the time you got real mad at each other.'

He went on. 'You've been thinking about that, I'd say.' He paused again. 'Sooner we clear the air, the better.'

Ellie nodded again, half-frightened, half-relieved.

The old man cleared his throat. 'Well-ll, that was it. We argued, about a lot of things. God did we argue! But mostly about her marrying like that, and taking off. I ...' he paused and started again, his voice gruff and almost loud. 'Well, I never got on with your dad.

That's no secret. I never trusted him and I told him so. Seemed to me he didn't want a family. I suggested Mags come back here and bring the pair of you. She got really mad. I can't blame her.'

Ellie sat silently. She didn't know what to say. She'd successfully blanked her dad out of her memory. He'd hardly ever been around, anyway. Grandpa had been right about him not wanting a family.

Grandpa frowned. 'Davey was only a baby. Your mother and I yelled at each other. She told me to stay out of her life. I got on my high horse, clammed up and stormed off!' He eyed Ellie. 'It's our stupid pride see … don't like anyone else telling us what to do.'

Ellie knew all about that. She swallowed and whispered, 'What happened?'

The old man got up and took his cup to the sink, turning his back so she couldn't see his face. 'Just that. We did stay out of each other's lives. We stopped writing, stopped being close. I gave away all her things. The longer it went on, the worse it got.' He stared, unseeing, out of the kitchen window. After a while he went on. 'She was my only child. I'd cared for her since she was a wee baby, when her mother died.' His voice cracked and he said sharply, 'Now she's gone.'

Ellie knew the sharpness wasn't because Grandpa was cross. He was hurting like her. She hadn't thought of Grandpa's pain or that he was feeling the same black ache as she was. She tried to say something but her lips were too stiff.

He cleared his throat and continued. 'Not long after Davey's first birthday, when your dad took off, I rang, but,' he sighed, 'I handled it badly. She thought I was saying "I told you so." I wasn't, but she told me to get lost, and I did.' He banged the bench top. 'I behaved like a fool again. Six wasted years. Six bloody wasted years! Now she's gone.' He stared down. 'I don't know whether I should be talking to you like this, but you asked, and you have a right to know. And we've all got to move on.'

There was a long silence. Ellie struggled to know what to say. Because it was family, she could see how it happened. They were all stubborn, even Davey. But adults could be even dumber than kids. Mum would never admit Grandpa was right about their dad. And somehow Grandpa should have done more to fix that. Ellie sighed. He was probably right. It wasn't any use going on about it now. She took another deep breath, trying to get the words to come.

Davey beat her to it. 'Don't cry Grandpa,' he whispered from under the table, his own voice heavy with tears. 'Mum would be glad we're together now.'

Ellie swallowed and muttered her agreement. 'Yeah. Davey's right, Grandpa. Mum would be glad we're here — not with Welfare.' Then she flushed and added, 'She really loved Larsen's Point. She kept that picture of you and her and the fish.'

'Yeah,' Davey emerged from under the table. 'In that old album. You and Mum had a fish. A great big fish. We had one like that too. Ellie showed me.'

The old man shook his head and laughed sadly. 'That one, eh? That old bald chin groper. A real beauty. Mags was fifteen.'

'I'm going to catch a bald chin groper one day, I bet,' announced Davey.

Ellie sat thinking about Mum here, in this strange old house. The pictures in the album showed her growing-up years — a life Ellie had only guessed at before. She wanted to ask about the seal, and some of the girls, and the tall dark-haired boy, then decided against it. In time Grandpa might share all his memories with them. Right now she couldn't take any more.

13

The talk about Mum did seem to clear the air. After that, when they sat eating their meals round the kitchen table, Grandpa often told them things that happened as Mum was growing up. About her friends and times at school, about her chooks and silkworm collection and her passion for The Beatles. One evening she followed him out onto the verandah. 'Well?' he said. He didn't even look up from his charts. He just knew she was there.

Ellie took a deep breath and said, 'What did Mum find out about the scratchings, Grandpa?'

He looked at her over his spectacles. 'I thought you'd get back to that. What makes you think I know anything different from what I've already told you?'

Ellie fidgeted with a bit of fishing net. 'What you said about asking the local Aboriginal fellas. You wouldn't have done that if you thought there was nothing to it.'

He gave a dry laugh. 'I thought you'd picked that up. It's my job to chat to those blokes about a lot of things.' Then he frowned and sighed. 'And if there *is* more to the scratchings, what then? Have you thought about that? You go stirring up the same bees' nest Mags did, and it'll mean a whole lot of so-called experts coming down here — arguing, changing the place, bringing tourists.'

Ellie hadn't thought of that. 'I don't want to change anything. It's just,' she glanced up, excitement making her stomach squeeze, 'it's such a fantastic mystery. I can't stop thinking about it, about who carved those letters and why. There must be other clues. Maybe ...'

Grandpa snorted. 'Maybe, maybe, maybe. Believe you me, *if* there is a secret, no one's found it yet — and, there's been plenty looking. *And* ... *if* by some crazy chance you do find something, it doesn't belong to you, you know. It belongs to the whole town, the whole country. And that means publicity.'

'You mean, if I ... if someone, were to discover more clues, everyone would have to know?'

'Oh yes. You can't hide something like that.' Then he shrugged. 'For my money, you won't find anything more than a pile of seaweed like the rest of us. So you may as well go ahead and look. If you find anything, good luck to you.' He cocked an eyebrow at her, and Ellie knew he was half teasing when he added, 'For the sake of peace and quiet I'll tell you what I know.'

Ellie sank onto the seat next to him. The old man stared out at the fading clouds and flashing beam, and said, 'You were right. Some folk round here, including me, used to think the L was for Larsen, that the figures were scratched there long before the house was built.' He laughed shortly. 'That's only what some folk think. And as I told you, I was ordered to pull my head in.'

Ellie shook her head. 'They must have been brain-dead. What happened then?'

He peered at her over his spectacles and frowned. 'You want all the details, don't you?'

She wasn't scared off at all. 'Yes please.'

He snorted, and taking off his glasses began to polish them. 'Let's see. When I first came here, way back forty years ago now, I got excited about those scratchings. There were records and so on about the Irish convicts, but the *O.S.L. 1756* ... nobody was saying anything about that. I thought ...' he stopped and snorted again. 'Anyway, I reported it to Head

Office and they sent a fella out here.' He shook his head. 'Some city fella supposed to have a lot of fancy letters after his name. He poked around and said it was a lot of fuss about nothing. That kids must have done it.'

'Sooo-o, what did you do?' Ellie just knew Grandpa wouldn't have accepted the official ruling.

'Why should I do anything?' He glared at her and rubbed his nose. After a while he muttered, 'Actually, I got an old mate of mine from the university down here and he took a good look at them too.'

'Well?'

He shrugged. 'Well, like you, he reckoned kids wouldn't have done those carvings. And he made a lot of other tests to find out how long they'd been there. Checked some records and so on.'

'And?'

'He thought it possible the date and the O.S.L. were real. That someone had scratched them there when it was just a cave, before the main lighthouse was built in 1850.'

'Wow! What did you do?'

Grandpa frowned. 'Like a fool, I sent a copy of his report to Head Office.'

'Didn't they believe it?'

'They rubbished the report and reprimanded me for wasting time — it was more than my job was worth to go on about it.'

'Why?' Ellie was outraged.

'In those days people weren't so aware of heritage. Nor fussy about it either. Conserving old things wasn't considered important, just expensive. Government departments are more careful nowadays.' He grunted again. 'Not necessarily more sensible or knowledgeable, or more ready to spend money, but more careful.'

'So that was it?'

'As far as Head Office was concerned, it was.' The old man shook his head again. 'They found out later that the first inspector was a bit of a phoney. It had already embarrassed some top johnny in the government no end. So they hushed it all up.' He shrugged. 'Actually it was no skin off my nose. As I said, I never wanted a whole bunch of smarty-ass professors phaffing round the place, getting in my hair.'

'Is that when you asked the local Aborigines?'

'That's right. The old blokes from round here reckoned Larsen was the name of a fella marooned here long ago. Tribal stories say a white man's ship was caught in a mighty storm, just off the point there. One of the seamen was washed overboard, and the ship beat it out to sea to avoid the rocks. They never did come back. Only the one man was washed up, just alive — no other survivors. There was a lot of other wreckage, so the ship might have gone down too.' The old man fitted his glasses back on his nose. 'Anyway that's their story.'

'And that was Larsen?'

'If you accept the Aboriginal talk, it could have been. It's a bit like Olaf's stories. Nobody has proved anything, and officially the story doesn't exist.'

'Do you believe it?'

The old man frowned and looked away. 'I told you, it doesn't matter what I believe. But I'll say this: the old fellas usually know what they're talking about. I'd believe them before that idiot they sent to check it out. Still,' he shrugged, 'as I said, it's too late now, and probably all hogwash, anyhow.' Then he added, as though he were trying to convince himself, 'Besides, most of those early ships were Dutch as far as we know, and Larsen was Swedish.'

Ellie nodded slowly. Now Grandpa'd actually started talking, she wanted to keep him going. She smiled and said encouragingly, 'We learned about the Dutch explorers.'

'Yes, well it's hard enough to trace shipping lists

from fifty years ago, let alone over two hundred and fifty years. Records are patchy. My mate did try. When he was in Holland a year later, he dug out a copy of the map those sailors would have used. And he checked records in Amsterdam.'

'Did he find anything?'

The old man snorted. 'Want chapter and verse, don't you? A Dutch ship, called *Leeuwenhoek*, after a Dutch scientist at the time, could have been lost in this area in the spring of 1756. But Larsen wasn't on the original crew list. He could have signed on at the Cape of Good Hope of course. The ship never made it to Batavia and it was assumed she'd been wrecked on the coast of the Great Southland — like so many before her.'

Ellie nodded. She'd heard about that at school. Lots of the early sailing ships missed their mark and were blown onto reefs along the west coast. Remains of Dutch wrecks kept turning up all the time. 'So you think Larsen was on the *Leeuwenhoek*?'

Grandpa shrugged. 'Did I say that? Who knows — or will ever know? Some sailors always died of ship fever and the Dutch captains took on crew from everywhere, mostly the Cape. Then they followed the "wagon way" to the Spice Islands. Maybe Larsen was on board. A whole lot of "could haves" there.'

Ellie pictured the scene. The sailor dredged up from the sea, lying down there on the sand of Our Beach. 'What happened then?' she whispered.

'According to local Aborigines, their ancestors nursed this bloke back to life, but he was like a dead man walking. He lived with them and camped right up on the point there, always hoping to be rescued. They say he used to stare out to sea, waiting and waiting for a ship that never came.'

'And that's why it's called Larsen's Point.' Ellie shivered. She could almost feel the man's despair and loneliness. 'Sheesh.' She stared out at the black line of the vast Southern Ocean, flicked every few seconds by the regular flash from the lighthouse. There'd be no friendly light for Larsen, just thousands of miles of dark empty sea between him and his homeland. She imagined him waiting, day after day, until all hope died. She shuddered. 'So no one ever came for him?'

Grandpa shrugged. 'Who'd know where to find him? All his shipmates dead. His ship wrecked. He must have died a lonely death somewhere — not far from here, I guess. Poor devil.'

'Has anyone ever found any stuff from the wreck, or anything?'

'Not that I know of. Old Micky Tuggle reckons his

grandpop used to talk of a cave, supposed to be Larsen's Cave where he collected everything he could find from the wreck …'

Ellie frowned. 'So you're talking about a different cave — not the one where the initials are carved?'

'It seems so. Remember there was no house here two hundred years ago, and *if*,' Grandpa leaned heavily on the word, '*if* there really was a Larsen, he would have wandered around all over the headland. He could have carved his name in a dozen different places.'

Ellie nodded reluctantly. 'I guess so.' She didn't want to let her theory go. 'But surely that cave — or maybe one of the others near the lighthouse …'

The old man shook his head impatiently. 'Not unless he could breathe underwater. That area is below sea level most of the time. Anyway, it's all a lot of make-up talk — amounting to nothing.'

'But …'

'No more now, lass. It's time for my news program.'

Ellie nodded. She had enough to go on for a while.

14

Later that week Ellie and Grandpa sat out on the verandah watching the moon rise and the lighthouse flash its message across a smooth sea. It had become a sort of evening ritual. Sometimes they talked, sometimes they just enjoyed the sea sounds and the sense of the earth settling down from the day.

The old man lifted his head and sniffed the air. 'No bad weather around. Good for the holiday sailors.'

Ellie had never seen the bay anything but mildly choppy. 'Does it get really rough, Grandpa?'

He snorted. 'That millpond out there can turn into a raging maelstrom with twelve metre waves — even at this time of the year. Can be nasty in a racing yacht.'

Far out to sea, the lights of a ship pricked the

darkness. The old man fumbled with his spectacles and checked the charts in his lap. 'That'd be the *Argosy Dan,* cargo freighter out of Bombay. She's on her way to Auckland.'

Ellie stared out to the horizon, imagining the captain marking off Larsen's Point on his charts. There really was a link between ship and shore. Her mind went back to the first Larsen. No warning light for him to steer by. The thought of that lonely sailor waiting and waiting, dreaming of home, haunted her. And 1756 — was that his first year? Or his last? Or maybe just sometime in between? And what about the rest of the stuff from the shipwreck. Where had he hidden it? In her mind's eye she saw him carefully hoarding each piece. Even the skeleton of a dead shipmate. She shuddered.

Beside her the old man grunted. 'Cat walked on your grave?' Ellie blinked. Mum often used the same dumb words. He laughed. 'It's an old saying meaning "have you been thinking spooky thoughts?"'

'I know that. Mum used to say the same thing,' Ellie shrugged. 'Actually, I was thinking about that Swedish sailor.' He hmmphed, ignoring the question in her voice. 'I was ... er ... wondering, if by some weird coincidence, the O.S. stands for Olaf something. Just like our Mr Larsen, now.'

Grandpa hmmphed again. 'I hope not, but it's possible.' And disappeared into his charts again.

Ellie wasn't going to let the subject drop. 'I was thinking about how he kept all that stuff from the wreck, and everything.' She cleared her throat and asked casually, 'Didn't Mum and what's-his-name turn up anything at all? I mean, you'd need a dry place not too far from the beach. Perhaps there are some of the caves near here ...?' her voice trailed off in the question.

The old man took off his glasses and glared at her. 'You know the answer to that lass. And what's-his-name is Michael Westway. Are you planning to keep talking right through the sunset?' She grinned at him. 'Mmmm-hmmm,' he sighed. 'Okay. Mags and that young Westway went over every square inch of the coast round here. If there was anything left to find, they'd have found it.' He glared at her. 'Don't you go crawling round sea caves. They can collapse without warning. Anyway,' he shrugged, 'there's nothing to find!'

'Who was Michael Westway, Grandpa? Was he the boy in Mum's album?'

'That'd be right. Mags and Mike were great mates. The Westways had a cottage just west — up the coast a bit. Came down every school holidays — year after year. Mags and Mike went everywhere together. Grew up together. I always thought ...' He stopped and shrugged.

Ellie held her breath, waiting. Grandpa seemed lost in his own memories. She cleared her throat, pressing for more. 'Do the Westways still come down?' At the back of her mind was the scrawl on the back of the strange drawing: *What do you think Mags? M.* Maybe it did all mean something.

The old man laughed shortly. 'That was years ago, child.' He shook his head and scowled. 'Mike became a pilot and had an accident, crop dusting. He took off then, over east somewhere. Ended up marrying his nurse. Mags was heartbroken.'

It was like hearing some terribly romantic story from a movie, but it was about Mum. 'Was he badly hurt?'

'Badly enough at the time — almost crippled. Had some crazy idea that he was no use to anyone like that. I heard he was gradually able to walk again. Never fly.' The old man frowned and shuffled his charts. 'He wrote to me once when Mags went off with your dad. I believe he already had a son himself by that time.' He hauled himself out of his chair, growling, 'Can't stop here yapping all night. I've got reports to make.'

Ellie stayed, curled up in the old basket chair. She guessed Grandpa had thought Mum and this Mike would marry some day. Things had turned out differently. She sighed, feeling somehow hurt and left out. Mum had never said a thing, never even mentioned the Westways or anything about her friends here. She was willing to bet that Michael Westway was the 'M' who'd made that drawing of the lighthouse. It all seemed so sad, so long ago.

Far out to sea the last of the lights from the *Argosy Dan* disappeared over the horizon.

15

A few days later, Grandpa went to see Olaf Larsen and came back with a couple of bikes. 'The Taylors are leaving town,' he said. 'Picked these two up in their garage sale.' He lifted the bikes out of the ute. They were a bit rusty and knocked about, but they seemed to work all right. Davey was off on the smaller one almost as soon as it hit the ground.

'Hey!' Grandpa called. 'Back-up there young fella. The tyres need air.'

Davey wobbled back and squatted down, workmanlike, to inspect the wheels. 'I'll help you fix 'em, Grandpa. I'll fix Ellie's too.'

Grandpa grinned. 'Well, lad, they might need a spot of oil and grease here and there, not to mention paint.'

'Okay,' beamed Davey. 'I'll paint. I might even be a bike painter one day.'

Grandpa closed his eyes. 'Now why did I think you'd say that? Well what colour?'

'Red!' they all shouted together.

As it turned out, they painted Ellie's blue with some of the paint from Mr Larsen's store. Davey painted his a bright pillar-box red. He gave it about ten coats and had to wait two days for it to dry properly.

'Ohhhh,' sighed Davey, when he could finally stroke his shiny machine. 'Grandpa I bet it's the fastest, best bike in the world. I bet!'

'That's some bet, Davey,' said Grandpa. 'I'm glad you like it.'

Ellie went pink in the face and murmured, 'Thanks Grandpa. It's … they're really neat. The kids who lived next door had bikes.' Then added without thinking, 'Mum was going to get us new ones when we'd saved up enough.'

The old man frowned and looked down. 'Well, yes. Let's say these are part of that promise.' He had his fierce look on again. 'You'll need them to ride up to the bus-stop, when you start school.'

Ellie flushed. Why did he look so fierce? Maybe Grandpa was worrying about money?

He eyed them both, 'Now, look after your machines properly. Check the tyres and the oil, clean 'em regularly. Salt and sand mess up the works. And don't forget what I said: you can ride the tracks around here, as long as you keep the lighthouse in sight.'

He sounded really mad. Ellie thought she must have said the wrong thing or something. She wanted to say 'sorry' but she didn't know how or why.

Davey wasn't put off in the least. 'Thanks Grandpa,' he hooted and zoomed off down the track, Nibs barking madly beside him. Ellie hung around uncertainly, then followed him.

That evening, she cooked dinner of chops, mashed potatoes and fresh garden peas. She hoped she did all right — like Mum would have. 'Okay?' she asked shyly.

Grandpa stared at her from under his brows, then nodded. 'Just about my favourite meal,' he said.

'Can I pick my bones?' mumbled Davey, slipping gristly bits to Nibs under the table.

'It's time we talked about school,' said Grandpa. 'That's one of the reasons I got the bikes. Holidays end in about six weeks. We should think about that.'

Ellie wasn't sure she wanted to think about school yet. She'd shoved the thought to the back of her mind. School reminded her of Shelley, of all the people she knew there, and the old life. Things were so neat at Lighthouse Cottage. It was so peaceful and safe with just the three of them. They were in a world of their own, the days drifting by, exploring the house, the reef, the beach … It was all she wanted right now.

'I start high school this year,' she said slowly, pushing her chop around the plate.

Grandpa nodded. 'I know. Larsen District High goes from Year One up to Year Ten. After that there's Fitzgerald Senior High.'

Ellie didn't say anything. She felt slightly sick. Explaining things to strange kids and strange teachers would be gross. What if she started to cry or something? That'd be the worst. Tears came when she least expected them. Most of the time she was okay, but when she had to talk about Mum and stuff the sadness just welled up inside of her. Imagine if she started bawling at a new school!

The old man eyed her sharply. 'Does school worry you, girl?'

Ellie shrugged. 'I just wondered if there was correspondence for out here, or something like that.' She tried to sound casual. 'Some of the station kids near Shelley had School of the Air. Davey and I could do correspondence here together.'

'Yeah,' breathed Davey. He had no fixed ideas about school, but he didn't want to change anything either.

The old man eyed them steadily. 'You and Davey will still be together at Larsen District High.'

Ellie moved her chair uneasily and shrugged again. 'I just thought it'd be cool to try something like School of the Air.' She wasn't going to tell Grandpa she found the thought of high school totally scary.

He seemed to guess anyway. 'It's no good burying yourself out here,' he said, almost gently. 'A new school may seem tough at first, but you'll get past that. Thinking's worse than doing.' After a pause he muttered, 'I'll be here to help, lass.'

Ellie sighed and nodded. If she wasn't going to end up a total loser, she'd have to go to high school. 'Nah. I guess it's cool,' she murmured.

'Anyway,' Grandpa scowled. 'We've no choice. Welfare are still on our backs.'

Ellie screwed up her nose, remembering the Welfare lady's grim promise to 'check up about the schooling'. Well, if she and Davey had to go, they had to go. 'Yeah,' she muttered. 'I guess so.' Why was she being such a drag about it — she'd have to meet other kids sometime. She sighed and asked, 'Do you know who my teacher'll be?'

He shook his head. 'Someone new I think. Mrs Parsons is the Year Two teacher. Nice enough woman — said she was looking forward to meeting Davey.'

'I just hope whoever I've got is not used to mega-geniuses or anything.'

The old man fixed an eye on her. 'Just do your best lass — nobody's going to expect a genius. If it doesn't work out we'll think of something else.' Ellie felt a little better. Grandpa would always be on their side.

Davey was thinking hard, swinging his legs back and forwards. 'Did Mum have to go to school, Grandpa?'

'Mags caught the bus into school. Just like you will. The driver called her the lighthouse kid. I guess you'll be the lighthouse kids too.'

Davey grinned, happy with this definite social advantage. 'I bet everyone wishes they were lighthouse kids. I bet.' Then he frowned. 'But only kids go to school, Grandpa. That's not fair. Why *do* only kids have to go to school?'

The old man buttered a slice of bread and flicked a glance at Davey. 'Everybody goes to school, son. Even me, in my day.'

Davey's eyes opened wide. 'Really? Here? In Larsen's Point? Last year?'

Ellie saw the twinkle in Grandpa's eye as he said,

'Hundreds of years, and miles away, on the other side of the world. But,' he stacked up the plates, 'schools are pretty much the same everywhere, any time, and all kids have to go to them.'

Davey screwed up his nose. 'Yeah,' he said, then smiled and added, 'but we got bikes.'

16

Later that evening, on the verandah, Ellie shuffled about, fidgeting and trying to get her words sorted out. The old man watched her pace up and down, scratch at the paintwork and change position a dozen times.

After a while he said. 'Have y'got something on your mind lassie — or are y' just practising to be a cricket?'

Ellie wriggled and collapsed into the old basket chair. She wanted to tell him it was all right about school and everything. And that they could really do without the bikes if cash was short, but she didn't want to get him all heated up, like this afternoon. Eventually she blurted out, 'The bikes are really cool, Grandpa, but we don't have to have them if they're too expensive or anything. We can walk to the bus.

Davey's going ape like that because we never had our own bikes before.'

The old man clicked his tongue. 'Oh so that's what's worrying you.' He snorted and shook his head. 'And you thought I was mad at you. It's not the cash, lass. They hardly cost me anything. It's just I keep thinking of ways I should have helped your mother — like get you bikes. I was such a fool.'

'We were okay,' Ellie mumbled, and stared at her hands in her lap. After a while she said, 'Tell me more about Mum growing up here and everything.'

He laughed wryly and sighed. 'Oh, they were good times. And though it was just Mags and me at the cottage, and I was busy most of the day, she never seemed lonely. She really did love it here — knew the whole place like the back of her hand.'

Ellie thought of all those years her mum had spent away from the sea, away from Larsen's Point. She and Davey had only been here a short while and already she couldn't think of living anywhere else. Mum must have really missed it all. 'Did Mum know you owned Lighthouse Cottage forever?'

'She knew.'

'I wish ...' Ellie's voice trailed off. She couldn't bring herself to say she wished Mum had brought them back here. It'd be sort of disloyal, like saying their time at Shelley wasn't good enough.

Grandpa frowned. 'Yeah, well, we can't change things now. It's no use wishing for the moon.'

Ellie winced, remembering Mum using the same words — only at Shelley, 'wishing for the moon' usually meant wanting (but not having) the money to fix the car, or buy a new dress. She sighed. Grandpa was feeling bad too, but he was right. Wishing things were different was useless.

She brought the subject back to the pictures in the album. 'Tell me about the seal in that photo with Mum and you.'

The old man smiled faintly. 'Lucky — he was Mags' pet. He hung around here until he was full-grown. Used to wait down at Our Beach for her to go swimming with him.' He flicked his head, remembering.

'Does he still come back?' Ellie couldn't think of anything more wonderful than playing with a wild seal.

Grandpa shrugged. 'It was years ago. But seals and sea-lions, dolphins, different sorts of whales, all call in here. They've been stopping off at this headland for thousands, probably millions, of years on the way to their breeding grounds. People are the new johnnies here.'

'What happened to Lucky?'

The old man scowled. 'Orphaned. Dodgy fishing boats trespassed round here, breaking all the rules, dragging the sea floor for anything that moved — they even took sealskins.' He banged the side of the chair disgustedly. 'People like that'd do anything for a fast dollar. They used those nets called 'walls-of-death'. Dolphins and seals get tangled in them and drown. It was one of that mob that killed Lucky's mum.'

'That's gross! Couldn't you stop it?'

'Nobody in power really cared a lot in those days. When she was about fifteen, Mags and her mates started a campaign.'

'A campaign?'

'Yeah,' he grinned proudly. 'To make that sort of net-fishing illegal. They collected a thousand signatures and got the school to send a petition to the local MP.'

'What happened?'

'Ahhh,' he snorted in disgust. 'Not enough, but it was a start. It's different now. Illegal boats from all over still fish these waters, but if the Coastwatch find out, they're down here like a shot. It's part of my job to report them. You can keep your eyes skinned too.'

'Sure!' Ellie nodded angrily. The very thought of

greedy men killing the sea creatures made her wild. She wondered if she'd be brave enough to start a campaign. Grandpa must have been so proud of Mum. Ellie swallowed. What if she couldn't be like Mum? What if she disappointed Grandpa? She looked up quickly and found him watching her over the top of his glasses.

'I'd never compare you and Mags, Ellie. Don't ever think I mean that. The past is past. You can't repeat it. Not even here. You don't have to be anyone but yourself.'

She squirmed uneasily, not quite sure if he meant what she thought he meant. Had he known what she'd been thinking? 'It's just that with Mum growing up here — and now me. It's as though things were happening all over again.'

'Well, they're not.' His voice was all growly, but Ellie knew he wasn't mad. He went on, 'You're your own person. You're like your mum in some ways, but you're not her. Be yourself. You're a different person.'

Ellie gulped, lost for a reply. But it was what she needed to hear. Grandpa didn't want her to take Mum's place. Now she thought about it, she didn't even want to — especially if it meant doing stuff like fishing. She could learn all about Mum, but she would think her own thoughts. She flushed and muttered 'Okay,' and stared hard out to sea. The old man got up, patted her on the head, and went off to watch the news.

17

The next day, Ellie and Davey planned to take a packed lunch and explore on their bikes. Grandpa made them a mud-map and pointed out the safe beaches and the places he thought they should go.

It was his lamp-cleaning day and he wanted no interruptions. He came out of the dungeon loaded with cleaning materials, blinking, and pretending to be blinded by the startling red and blue bikes. 'They'll see you fifty ks out to sea on those machines,' he said. 'Now remember what I said: keep the lighthouse in sight.'

Nibs bounced up and down, snapping at the seagulls, ready for adventure. Off they went, the dog racing far ahead, then circling back to join them from behind.

They rode on, further west than they'd ever gone

before and still the lighthouse dominated the horizon. They stopped for a swim at a small cove like Our Beach. Nibs joined them, splashing into the crystal green water, scaring off a school of yellowtail.

Afterwards they sat on the warm sand and munched sausage sandwiches. 'I might be an explorer one day,' sighed Davey, adding, 'on a red bike, and I'd take Nibs.' Nibs rolled on his back in agreement.

Ellie smiled. Davey was going to have a busy life. 'C'mon. Let's see how far we go before we lose the lighthouse.' They crested the hill and looked down into a wide valley with green paddocks reaching almost to the beach line. A house was perched on the cliff over a small bay.

'There's someone there,' hissed Davey, dropping to his stomach like a Red Indian. Ellie and Nibs joined him, the dog panting hard, saliva rolling off his tongue.

A woman was hanging clothes on a line at the back of the cottage. A cat wound itself in and out her legs. Nibs sniffed once and took off in a beeline for the cat.

'Oh Jeez!' gasped Ellie. 'Nibs! Here!' she yelled, and got absolutely no response.

In a moment Davey was on his bike, wobbling flat out down the hill, calling 'Nibs! Nibs!' at the top of his voice. Ellie wasn't far behind. The cat took off up a drainpipe and vanished, Davey skidded and fell off at the woman's feet. Nibs jumped all over him, licking and barking and having a wonderful time.

'Hi. I'm Davey,' he said, picking himself up and frowning severely at Nibs. 'Nibs is a *bad dog!*' Nibs squirmed and apologised happily.

'I'm sorry,' murmured Ellie, as she arrived. 'He's not used to cats.'

The lady looked at her sharply. 'I can see that.' She was not amused. 'And poor Tuffy's not used to dogs.'

'Sorry,' gulped Ellie again, scowling at Nibs and half-slapping him on the back. '*Bad, bad dog!*' Nibs wriggled onto her foot, obviously not taking any of the 'bad dog' bit too seriously.

A door banged and a man limped out, leaning on a stick. 'No harm done, Freda. Tuffy's okay.' He smiled at Ellie and Davey, putting his hand down to scratch Nibs' ear. 'I had a border collie like this once.'

The woman rolled her eyes. 'There wouldn't need to be two of them,' she snapped, tossing sleek black hair from her face. Then she grabbed up the empty clothes basket and stomped inside.

'I'm Michael Westway,' the man smiled pleasantly, 'and you are …'

Ellie gasped. It was Davey who announced,

'Davey, Davey Flannagan.' He nodded over his shoulder. 'She's Ellie, and Nibs is the Bad Dog!' He glared at Nibs, again without any effect.

Ellie stared, trying to see the tall, dark-haired boy from Mum's album in the man before her. Grandpa said he'd had an accident. The walking stick almost proved who he was. He was watching her, a bit puzzled. 'Do I know you?' he asked.

Ellie flushed. 'No, sir. That is … I think you knew our mum.'

There was a long silence. Nibs collapsed, panting in a heap, with Davey beside him. The man studied her face. Finally he spoke. 'So you're Mags' children.' Ellie nodded silently. He poked the ground with his stick and muttered huskily, 'I heard what happened. It was …' He seemed to shake himself. 'I'm so terribly sorry.'

Ellie swallowed, fighting back tears. Davey lifted his head from Nibs' tummy. 'We live with Grandpa now. Do you know Grandpa?'

The man nodded. 'Oh yes, I know Hamish.' He looked sad. 'And long ago I knew your mother. She was a wonderful person.'

Ellie stood, kicking at the dirt, not knowing what to say. Finally she managed, 'I saw a picture of you in Mum's album.'

'There'd be a few of those. She was my best

friend.' Michael Westway looked over towards the lighthouse. 'We grew up together.' He glanced at Ellie. 'You are very like her.'

'Thank you,' whispered Ellie. She stared at the house and tried to make conversation. 'Do you live here now or are you visiting?'

The man grinned. 'We live here, full time these days.' He pulled a face. 'I'm slightly bashed up and it's good for my health, you see.' He glanced towards the house. 'Err-r would you like to come in, have some lemon squash or something ...'

'No thank you,' murmured Ellie. 'We're fine.'

'I would,' announced Davey. 'I like lemon squash.'

'No you wouldn't, Davey!' hissed Ellie, red in the face. 'We've just had lunch.' The lady called Freda would certainly not welcome them. She started to make leaving movements, calling Nibs to her, brushing off her jeans, apologising for Davey.

'It's all right,' said the man quietly. 'Perhaps we'll meet another day. I guess it's been a bit of a shock for all of us, right now.' He smiled. 'My son Aaron will be home next week. I'd like you to meet him. He must be about your age, Ellie, perhaps a year or two older — he's fifteen. He's a boarder at Scotch and he's on a school camp.'

Ellie swallowed. 'That'd be cool,' she said

politely. 'I'm sorry about Tuffy. I hope he's okay.'

Michael Westway grinned. 'Cats are always okay.'

Later, as they pushed the bikes back up to the track, Ellie wondered at the way things happened sometimes. Mum had been best friends with Mr Westway, now she was going to meet Aaron. It was kind of spooky.

When they got home Ellie told Grandpa about their meeting with Michael Westway. The old man snorted. 'I knew they came down for holidays.' He frowned. 'Finally decided to stay here for good, eh?'

Ellie heard the anger in his voice. 'Don't you like the Westways any more?'

The old man gave a resigned sigh. 'It happened before you were born. For a while I blamed Mike for Mags rushing off with your dad. Which, I agree, sounds pretty damn stupid, now. Anyway,' he looked up and smiled wryly at Ellie, 'all that business was long ago and best forgotten.'

Later, out on the verandah, she told Grandpa about Aaron coming back from camp. He nodded. 'It'll be good for you to meet some new people.'

Ellie was instantly suspicious. 'Why?'

'Because you can't hide away from life out here all the time. You should meet youngsters your own age. Bring you out of yourself.'

There'd be time enough to meet new kids when the term started. Ellie wrinkled her nose. Mr Westway seemed cool enough — but Mrs Westway was a hag. Besides, she didn't want 'bringing out of herself'. The whole thing smelled like a set-up. 'We'll meet kids at school,' she muttered.

'True, but if the Westways are our neighbours you should get to know them too.' There was no way Ellie wanted to change things. Living in this house with Davey and Grandpa was perfect for now. 'I don't need to meet him, do I? It seems kinda weird anyway.'

The old man eyed her thoughtfully. 'Because Mike Westway was your mother's special friend?' He shook his head. 'This boy's a different person. So are you. I told you that. You should meet him.' Ellie sat in silence. She didn't want different people in her life. Adults, even the best ones, got some dumb ideas sometimes, then everything got too heavy. She sighed. She was sure to meet Aaron and other kids eventually. May as well get used to the idea. She just hoped he didn't turn out to be a complete nerdo.

She shrugged and said, 'He won't want to hang out with us anyway. He's fifteen!'

Grandpa grinned. 'Quite in his dotage then, eh?' Ellie didn't know what dotage meant and she wasn't going to ask.

The old man put down his charts. 'Well, you may as well fill me in on the whole picture. How is Mike? Did you meet his wife?'

'Yeah,' Ellie squirmed and pulled a face. 'We sort of ran into Mrs Westway. She was pretty mad because Nibs chased her cat. She went ballistic!'

Grandpa raised his eyebrows but said nothing. Ellie went on, 'He seemed nice though. But he did walk with a stick, and he's living here 'coz it's good for his health. Aaron goes to *boarding* school!' She rolled her eyes.

'I see. Well I guess that suits him. Anyway it's not our business and we'll see what he's like when we meet him.'

18

It was Saturday, a week later, when a shiny new Jeep pulled up outside the cottage. Michael Westway climbed slowly out of the cab. As Grandpa met him at the door, Ellie found she was holding her breath. The two men stood looking at each other for several moments before Mike said something, Grandpa nodded and they shook hands slowly.

After a minute Mr Westway called out and the Jeep door slammed again. A boy, tall and lanky with red hair, slouched over to shake the old man's hand. Ellie saw Grandpa glance quickly at her and go to say something, but she turned away, suddenly embarrassed. Just then, Davey and Nibs erupted from around the back and everything became noisy and chaotic.

'Ellie!' Grandpa caught her eye this time and Ellie

shambled over to greet Mr Westway. She was careful not to look at the boy until his father said, 'And this is Aaron. He's back from that camp I told you about.'

He was nothing like his father, except perhaps the dark eyes and sort of twisted smile. Ellie thought he looked like someone who lived inside himself and had things he didn't want to talk about. She mumbled, 'Hi,' and the boy raised his palm in an awkward half-wave. After that they stood around in silence while the two older men spoke of times past and what had happened since. Ellie knew Mr Westway wanted to say something about Mum and was horrified to find she was close to tears. She moved away, pretending to try and quieten Nibs and Davey.

'And now,' Grandpa had followed them, 'I've got these two young rapscallions to keep in line.'

Ellie fiddled with Nibs' collar and Davey asked, 'What's a rapscall ... what you said Grandpa?'

'A rascal, little matey,' growled the old man. 'Someone who asks questions all the time.' He pretended to cuff Davey round the head. 'But I reckon I'll survive you two anyway.' He looked across at Ellie. 'Mike tells me Aaron's going to be down for the rest of the holidays, Ellie.'

What was she supposed to say to that? She glanced quickly at Aaron who had squatted down to play with Nibs' ears. Nibs was getting so much attention he'd be off the planet soon. Ellie smiled weakly, 'Ohhh,' she mumbled, 'neat,' and then could have bitten her tongue.

Aaron didn't say anything, and Mr Westway began talking for him. 'Aaron has to collect specimens for a science project, so he'll be glad of some help.' Ellie could have died. Hadn't adults any idea how much embarrassment they caused? As if a high school kid of fifteen would want to hang around with a (nearly) Year Eight and her baby brother. She mumbled something unintelligible and wandered over to look at the sea.

Davey had no such qualms. 'Hey neat, Aaron. Me and Ellie know heaps of places. I found a sea-dragon yesterday. Grandpa told me — a leafy sea-dragon.' He beamed. 'And I can swim real well now.'

'Cool,' murmured the older boy. 'A leafy sea-dragon, eh?'

With her back to them all, Ellie rolled her eyes and blushed for her entire family.

19

Mike Westway took to driving over most days and chatting with Grandpa. Sometimes Aaron came too, but mostly he took off by himself on his bike. Ellie tried to make sure she and Davey had already gone by the time the Westway Jeep arrived. It wasn't that she thought Aaron was a loser or anything, she didn't even know him, but the thought of him being trapped into babysitting them really galled her. Besides, she suspected Grandpa and Mr Westway were trying to 'bring her out of herself' — or something.

Occasionally the Westways came early and there was nothing she could do about it. Then the three of them would spend an awkward couple of hours turning over rocks and poking through piles of wrack on the cliff. The last time they'd actually played cricket. She'd nearly died of embarrassment, though Davey was ecstatic and Aaron didn't seem to care one way or the other.

Ellie wasn't sure what she thought about Aaron. It was all mixed up with being dumped on him and wanting to vanish into a monster earth-hole. He never talked much, just loped around outside somewhere doing his own thing. He seemed to prefer Lighthouse Cottage to his place (Ellie could understand that), and he was patient with Davey.

As for Davey, he was Aaron's biggest fan. Aaron was cool! Aaron could swim like a fish! Aaron could kick a neat football and bowl a googly. Aaron was going to be a marine biologist. So was Davey, one day.

About a week after they'd met, Davey raced Ellie down a track into a small cove and let out a whoop of recognition. 'Hey Aaron! We're here! Ellie and me'll help you.'

'Davey!' Ellie tried to back up her bike. 'C'mon. He doesn't need us. C'mon.'

Davey stuck out his lip. 'He does so. We could help him collect specimens. I bet I'll find another leafy dragon.' He was torn between giving Aaron his treasure and finding another one. He raised his voice. 'I'm going to find you a sea-dragon like mine, Aaron. I bet I will.' And he jumped off his bike and ploughed down the sand-hill on to the beach. Ellie sighed and followed.

Aaron had been checking weed piles along the shore. He stood squinting into the sun. 'G'day Davey,' he muttered and nodded silently at Ellie. It was still early and the sweep of reef stood high above the tideline. Deeper pools glistened greenly between the weed-covered rocks. 'I'm just going to see what's out there,' he said quietly. 'If you're coming, don't pick up anything until I check it.' Ellie wasn't going to argue though she felt like it. Davey followed on Aaron's heels out across the reef, Ellie trailing along behind.

In most parts the water was still ankle-deep and tiny fish darted in and out of pink and brown weed into the deeper pools. She squatted down to watch a soft speckled snail-like creature glide slowly across a rock. The outer folds of its body floated gracefully like the skirts of a dancer. She drifted from pool to pool, entranced by the coloured weeds and shifting sea-life. Every now and then she heard Davey shout in excitement.

She had to admit it was a magic world. Gradually the tight knot of embarrassment inside her went away. She caught up with the two boys and the three of them splashed over the reef together, stopping every now and then as Aaron put down a gloved hand to pick up a creature or plant to add to his collection in the glass-bottomed bucket.

As they waded in closer to shore Aaron pointed out hundreds of red jelly-like blobs glistening across the entire underside of a rock ledge.

'What are they?' gasped Ellie. It was like something out of Aladdin's cave.

'Waratah anemones,' said Aaron. Davey put his finger into a circle of soft pink tentacles. They closed around him for a moment then sucked back and disappeared.

Ellie was too slow to stop him. 'Is that okay?' she asked. 'Aren't they poisonous?'

'Not much,' said Aaron. 'But it might hurt the anemone.' He shrugged. 'Sea animals feel pain like anything else. In any case, it's not a neat idea to touch things until you know what you're doing.'

Ellie churned inside. She could have thumped Davey but she said, 'I guess most of us aren't as smart as you. He won't do it again.'

The boy glanced at her quickly and flushed, but he didn't say anything. When they returned to shore, he tipped the contents of the bucket into a pool he'd dug in the sand and lined with black plastic. As the water settled, Ellie could see numbers of sea slugs, snails and minute fish. Tiny hermit crabs, with their borrowed shells, shuffled across the floor of the pool. As Aaron listed everything in a notebook, Davey burbled on about this specimen or that. Suddenly he reached down to pick up a highly-patterned cone shell.

'No!' Aaron almost shouted. 'Don't touch mate. I told you! Don't touch!' Davey froze and Ellie scowled, not knowing if she felt madder at Davey or Aaron. The older boy lowered his voice. 'It's got a poisonous barb, Davey,' he said, pointing. 'That's why y'gotta know what you're doing.'

Davey grinned. 'Okay.' But Ellie flushed, embarrassed again. Aaron was obviously sick of babysitting total boneheads like her and Davey.

'I think it's time we got going, Davey,' she muttered, and hauled him protesting away towards their bikes.

When she looked back, Aaron was staring out to sea, skimming small rocks across the incoming tide. Well, thought Ellie, that's it.

20

To Ellie's surprise, Aaron turned up at the lighthouse again the next day.

'Well, if you kids are off specimen hunting,' said Mike Westway, as Aaron lifted a bike out of the Jeep, 'you'd better get going before it gets too hot.'

Ellie swallowed. How'd that been decided? She couldn't imagine Aaron suggesting it. She desperately hoped it wasn't some scheme Grandpa and Mr Westway had cooked up. When Aaron got closer, she muttered, 'Look, it's cool. You don't have to drag us round. We can look after ourselves.'

He shrugged. 'Suit yourself. I've got to collect specimens anyway and the little bloke said he wanted to come.' He kicked the ground, slightly red in the face. 'I won't yell at you. Anyway, there's nobody else around, so you might as well.' Ellie wasn't sure whether he was apologising for yesterday or suggesting that she and Davey were his last choice. Maybe his dad had made him promise to take them or something.

Davey didn't care. He was delighted to join in. 'Hey, yeah!' he shouted. 'We're collectors.' Then, ever hopeful, 'We're going to find another sea-dragon, Grandpa. I bet.'

'I just bet you are, young fella,' grinned Mike Westway.

Grandpa ruffled the little boy's hair and glanced at Ellie. 'You have a problem, lass?'

Ellie flushed. She couldn't object any more without sounding like a real nerdo. 'No,' she muttered. 'It's cool.'

Shortly afterwards they set off loaded with lunch, hats, sunscreen and swimming gear. They went east this time, to a headland that she and Davey had never reached before. Davey raced down to the beach and Ellie went up to Aaron, determined to say her piece. He was unpacking his gear.

'Look,' she said, 'this collecting thing. You don't have to be stuck with us.'

He stared at her silently then clipped his notebook to his belt. After a moment he shrugged. 'I dunno,' he muttered. 'It's Dad's idea to get me out of the house, which is cool by me. If you want to come that's also cool — Davey seems to like the idea. But,' he banged sand clear of the bucket, 'suit y'self. I'm not in a sweat one way or the other.'

Ellie wished she hadn't been so full on. Aaron acted all laid back. It sounded like he knew his dad was trying on a scheme. Perhaps he really didn't care. Maybe it had something to do with his sour-grouch mum. Trying for a cooler attitude, she mumbled, 'Pretty gross having to do an assignment over the holidays.'

He shrugged again and squatted down to check his gear. She had turned to leave when he said, extra casually, 'What d'you know about this cave thing?'

'Cave thing?'

'Yeah,' he took out his knife and began cleaning it. 'Dad's told me about this cave your mum and he were looking for. Sounds really neat.'

'Larsen's Cave?' Ellie was trying to catch up on her thoughts. 'Yeah … well … there's no actual proof he even existed. I mean it could all be kid's stuff.'

Aaron stood, slinging his gear over one shoulder and picked up the bucket. 'Is that what you think?'

It was Ellie's turn to shrug. 'Well, Mum and your dad never found anything did they?'

They trudged beachwards. Suddenly Aaron muttered. 'Dad's made a topographical survey of the area, and there're stacks of caves around. Larsen's could be any one of them. I've got a copy of his map.'

His voice had changed — he couldn't disguise his interest. Maybe that was why he was so cool about them joining him. He must have been thinking about it for a while. She felt a surge of excitement. Two of them looking would make a huge difference. She asked just as casually, 'What've you heard about Larsen, then?'

Aaron hunched a shoulder. 'Not that much. Old Mr Larsen at the store goes on about his ancestors, but that's just talk.' He glanced at her sideways. 'Dad's told me some.' He grimaced. 'Like I said, I gotta do this marine life project anyway, so we might as well check out the cave thing too. It'd be really neat to find some evidence.'

Ellie ploughed through the sand. If Aaron was with them, Grandpa would let them explore further. And a topographical survey would show rock contours you wouldn't notice otherwise. And Aaron seemed to know what he was talking about too. Three good reasons to go with the idea. Besides, reef walking and snorkeling were cool. As long as Davey didn't stuff up, that is. 'Okay,' she said. He nodded and strode off towards the waterline.

The bay was really a lagoon formed from a

collapsed sea cave. They swam through deep ravines encrusted with soft corals, crimson and yellow sponges and drifting weed. Davey splashed ahead of them sending schools of bream and zebra fish darting into the deeper waters of the outer reef. Closer to shore they watched Aaron dive below overhanging ledges checking for hidden sea caves. He brought up the subject again as they warmed themselves on sun-smoothed rocks at the edge of the beach. 'Dad told me about some scratchings on the cave wall. It'd be really neat to see them.'

'They're in the dungeon,' yawned Davey, nearly asleep. 'It's horrible dark down there. They can chain you up in the dungeon.'

'Oh yeah?'

Ellie wrinkled her nose. 'Well, Davey is sort of right. It is a dungeon and there are chains. It's quite weird. And there's this scratching that says *O.S.L. 1756.*'

Aaron sat up. 'Is it for real?'

'Well-ll,' Ellie hesitated. 'It might be, but …'

'But what? Is it dodgy or something?'

Ellie shrugged. 'Nobody's certain.' She glanced sideways. 'The date 1756 is ages before anyone from Europe was supposed to know about Australia. *If* it is a date. It could be a convict number.'

Aaron screwed up his nose. 'What does your grandpop say?'

'Well,' Ellie sat up, 'Grandpa's pretty toey about it. He reckons he goes with the convict idea.' And she went on to repeat the facts and the maybes as Grandpa had told them to her. 'So the official line is that the carvings were done by convicts or kids fooling around.'

Aaron worked away at a shell stuck in the rock. 'What do you reckon?'

Ellie shook her head. 'Convicts could've, I guess. They built the lighthouse. But I reckon the carving's too good to be kids. And besides, the local Aborigines told Grandpa the place had been called something like Larsen even before European settlement.'

'So who was this guy?'

Ellie shrugged. 'Well, Grandpa thinks he may have been a Swedish sailor that got on a Dutch ship. The ship could have been the Leeuwin … something. It stopped at the Cape of Good Hope. That's at the bottom of Africa.'

'I know.'

Ellie went pink. Of course he'd know that. Probably thought she was trying to sound like an egghead, or something. 'Yeah well. That's about it.'

He flicked the shell away. 'Like I said, I heard Dad and your mum turned the coast upside down and never found anything.'

'Our mum's dead,' mumbled Davey.

'I heard that too.' Aaron's eyes met Ellie's. 'Sorry.'

She nodded, not trusting herself to speak, and hoping like crazy she wasn't going to make a bawling freak of herself. He didn't say anything more for a while. Ellie scratched at a limpet on the rock then stared out to sea.

Later he asked, 'So is it worth it to keep looking? I mean have you ...' He flicked his head at the cliffs behind them.

Ellie grinned weakly. 'Yeah, sort of. Grandpa says there's nowhere else to look, but I have been anyway. There're stacks of caves around.' She flushed, realising that he must know that too and added hurriedly, 'Even the cottage is full of caves and stuff. Have you seen inside the cottage?'

He snorted, flicking a strand of lank red hair from his eyes. 'You kidding? I've been hanging out, wanting to see the place. But,' he shrugged. 'Dad didn't seem to think it was a cool idea to ask. He thought it might upset your grandpop or something.'

Ellie wriggled uneasily. 'Well, I think he was sort

of mad at your dad for awhile.' She wriggled uncomfortably, 'But he's chilled out now. He's not nearly as fierce as he looks.'

Aaron nodded. Then he said, 'Okay. So it's a deal then. We keep looking.'

Ellie nodded. 'Okay,' she murmured.

'Me too,' from a sleepy Davey.

The older boy got up and looked back at the lighthouse on the landward horizon. 'Who'd want to be that poor guy Larsen,' he muttered.

'Yeah,' agreed Ellie, 'hanging around on a beach, all on your own — until you died.'

Aaron shook his head. 'Nobody'd even know whether he was alive or dead.' He shook his head again and muttered, 'He'd just be sitting there, waiting — for nothing! Like he never existed. Sheesh! Like being dumped in space.'

That day was the beginning of a different sort of time for Ellie. Where it had been only Grandpa, Davey and herself, now there was Aaron and Mr Westway as well. It meant new people in her life, new things to do, new things to think about. The dark pain inside her eased a little more.

21

Every morning Aaron marked out a different part of the coast to explore, and despite her early reluctance, Ellie looked forward to their daily excursions. To start with, she had to admit that beachcombing took on a new meaning. Aaron knew the name of every shell, crab, slug and anything else they turned up along the shoreline. He kept careful records, returning the live animals to the sea and sorting the rest in one of Grandpa's back sheds.

They got back to the shed early one afternoon and spent time classifying shells and painting special ones with baby oil to preserve their colours. Davey sat under the table with Nibs, riffling through his own very smelly box and sniffing each specimen happily. Grandpa stuck his head in the door, rolled his eyes and backed out again hurriedly.

'Don't you like our maritime museum,' Ellie called after him.

'Pretty smelly one, if you ask me,' he grumbled, and went off to check his instruments.

The sun was low on the horizon. Swirls of cloud changed colour across a huge expanse of sky. As it often did, the end of the day and the sense of the world turning made Ellie feel sad. For once even Aaron seemed restless. He stared out the shed door at the outline of the old cottage against the sea and murmured, almost wistfully, 'This is a great house. I wish ...'

Ellie looked up. 'Yeah?'

He shrugged, picking up a paper nautilus, lifting it high so the light glowed through the delicate curves.

'Dad's got an ace one of these,' he said. 'He told me your mum gave it to him years ago.'

'They were really good friends,' Ellie murmured.

She didn't like to say anything more. Except for that once on the beach, conversations hadn't got really personal. Aaron knew Mum was dead, and that was why she and Davey lived with Grandpa. But he'd never said what he thought about their parents being such close friends when they were kids.

He stared down at the nautilus for a moment then

laughed a short embarrassed laugh. 'It's like we should be related, isn't it?'

Ellie was lost for words. He almost sounded as though he wished he lived at the lighthouse and really was part of their family. 'Yeah,' she mumbled again and wondered about Aaron's mother. She seemed such a snake. How could Mr Westway have ever married her?

Mike Westway wandered in. 'You ready, Aaron? We'd better get home.'

Aaron grimaced and mumbled, 'In a minute, Dad.'

His father sorted through the specimens, picking out the same nautilus and holding it up to the light. 'My favourite shell, and what a beauty. Not a blemish anywhere.' He smiled wistfully at Ellie. 'Mags and I used to have a great collection,' he said.

Ellie didn't trust herself to speak, but Davey sensed the sadness in the older man's voice. 'Aaron told us. We can make another sea museum at your house, Mr Westway,' he offered kindly. 'And if we find another shell, you can give it to Mrs Westway and make her happy.' He didn't sound convinced.

Aaron stared at the ground and muttered, 'In your dreams.' Then he seemed to regret what he'd said and went outside. His dad frowned and limped after him.

Ellie glared at her brother. 'Shut up!' she mouthed. Davey had obviously hit a nerve. Aaron had never said anything bad about his mum before, even when she'd kicked them out the one other time they visited — again because of Nibs. Davey hadn't forgiven her. 'I bet marine museums are another thing the old bat doesn't like,' he muttered.

'Davey!' hissed Ellie. 'She's Aaron's mum.'

Aaron suddenly reappeared at the shed door. 'She's not my mum,' he said tightly, 'she's Freda Wetherington Westway — my father's second wife. And no, she doesn't like marine museums.'

'Right,' said Ellie fumbling for what to say next. Privately, she thought Aaron was lucky his real mum wasn't Mrs Freda Wetherington Westway — wow! What a mouthful!

He suddenly looked up and muttered, 'And it won't work out — doing this at my house, I mean. Does your grandpa really not mind if we keep storing things in this shed?'

'I'm sure he doesn't.'

Aaron was arguing something inside his head. 'I can set up a tent in my back yard. I've done it before.'

Ellie understood the feeling of not wanting to be obliged to someone, but she was certain Grandpa

didn't mind at all. 'Look it's cool. Not a problem —
really.' Being able to offer hospitality made her feel
good.

He nodded and muttered, 'See ya,' And went out
to the Jeep.

He really doesn't like to spend time at home,
thought Ellie. And maybe that was another reason
why Aaron put up with their company. He must
have felt awful about his stepmum kicking them out
of the house.

While she helped Grandpa get tea, Ellie thought
about Aaron and what he'd said about being related.
She'd never seen him lose his cool before. He wasn't
a wally or a creep or anything, he just didn't go on
about himself. Something must have really got into
him today. The business with his stepmum put her
definitely on his side.

But whatever was bugging him she and Davey
hadn't helped much. She sighed. She always felt bit
unco with boys — especially a boy like Aaron. He
didn't give much away and always turned up in a
floppy old hat and sunglasses so you couldn't see his
face. Most of the boys she'd known at Shelley were
real loudmouths. They hung around in a gang and
when any of the girls turned up, they'd fool about,
pushing and shouting. There'd been the usual

giggling and insulting on both sides, and a sort of jockeying around over who were girlfriends and boyfriends.

Ellie had always been too shy to get into that scene. She couldn't imagine Aaron in it either. He tended to keep himself to himself and didn't seem the sort for a big crowd. Probably had one or two friends who were pretty smart as well. Ellie grimaced. She wished she could be smarter and cooler. Well, at least she wasn't carrying on like an embarrassed idiot any more, and he seemed easier to talk to than when they'd first met.

Ellie cleared her throat. 'What d'you think of Aaron, Grandpa?'

He glanced sideways at her. 'Seems a nice enough young bloke. What about you?'

She shrugged. 'He's okay,' she said.

22

That evening, Ellie followed Grandpa onto the verandah at the usual time after dinner. He glanced up from his charts. 'Well?'

She curled up in the wicker chair. 'Grandpa, didn't you say Mr Westway married his nurse?'

'I did.'

'Well, Mrs Westway isn't Aaron's real mum.'

He stared at her for a moment before saying, 'Mike's first wife died not long after Aaron was born. A few years ago Mike married again — Freda Wetherington, daughter of a Queensland mining magnate.'

'Freda Wetherington Westway,' giggled Ellie. Everything seemed a little clearer to her now. Fancy calling yourself something like that. Poor Aaron, having her around every day. No wonder he was uptight and didn't like going home.

'That Mrs Thingabob Westway's an old bat!' Davey had followed Ellie out.

'And that's enough, young man!' rumbled Grandpa. Ellie looked away trying to keep a straight face.

'Well, she doesn't like Nibs,' announced Davey, quite unrepentant, his lower lip out, his eyes steely. 'Or me.'

'I don't blame her, young fella.' Grandpa's eyes were equally steely. 'Nobody likes rude little boys. *And* we don't make personal remarks in this family.' They glared at each other.

Finally Davey dropped his gaze and mumbled, 'No, sir,' adding quickly, 'she's not nice to Ellie either.'

Grandpa refused to meet Ellie's eyes. 'That's Mrs Westway's misfortune, my lad. Now let's forget about the lady.' He straightened Davey's pyjama pants. 'Bed for you, young fella,' he said, and sent him on his way with a pat on the backside.

When he'd gone, Ellie murmured, 'Davey's not far wrong, Grandpa. I don't think Aaron even likes her much.'

The old man sighed. 'I suspect Mike's an unhappy man, too. But it's not our business. So let's all mind our manners, eh?'

'Okay, but …'

'Yes?'

Ellie had a mass of unanswered questions, however, it was probably best to avoid ones about Mrs Westway for the moment. She cleared her throat. 'What does Mr Westway do?'

'Well, he can only work from his desk nowadays. He writes articles for technical magazines and he's an expert on ocean currents. All sorts of people use his knowledge.' Grandpa peered at her over his glasses. 'Anything else?'

Ellie grinned at him. He was pretending to be fierce again. She hadn't been fooled for a long time. 'Not at the moment,' she said and curled into her chair.

Grandpa gave a 'Hmmph!' and went back to his charts.

Ellie sat thinking about the changes in her life. Lighthouse Cottage was really home to her now. There was still the black ache every time she thought of Mum, but she was learning to live with that. She wondered what Aaron really thought about his stepmother. It must be awful living with someone you didn't like — all the time. If she had a stepmum like Mrs Westway, Ellie decided, she'd want to go to boarding school too.

She felt a sudden rush of thankfulness for Grandpa.

He might sound growly, even fierce sometimes, but she could always talk to him and get a straight answer. And, not that he'd ever said it, she knew she and Davey were important to him … 'This family,' he'd said. Ellie was glad she was part of 'this family'.

23

The weather held and the days slid one into the other. Every so often Ellie tried to 'free' Aaron from his babysitting duty. But he didn't seem to notice, and after a while the exercise seemed pointless. Each day they roamed farther up and down the coast, to steeper cliffs and wilder, lonely beaches. They often saw dolphins, seals too. Once they saw a large fishing boat moored off an island in a small bay, several kilometres east of the lighthouse.

'It's not supposed to be there,' muttered Aaron, screwing up his eyes against the glare.

Ellie remembered Grandpa telling her to keep an eye out for fishing vandals. 'Can you see the name?' she asked.

Aaron lay on his stomach and shaded his eyes. 'A ...' he managed. 'Double L, no! A-t-l — *Atlantis 3*.'

Just then a man came on deck and raised a pair of binoculars in their direction. He didn't shout or wave his arms or anything, but Ellie sensed hostility in the way he stood and stared at them. Davey suddenly jumped up and bent over, wiggling his bottom backwards and forwards in the man's direction.

'Davey!' hissed Ellie. It was a trick Davey had learned from one of his Shelley mates. Mum had hated it.

'Well, he didn't like us either,' snorted Davey, pink-faced and defiant.

Aaron grinned. 'And you showed him, didn't you mate.'

When they got home Ellie told Grandpa about the boat. 'What did you say it was called?' he asked.

'*Atlantis 3*. About seven kilometres east from here. Aaron said it shouldn't be there.'

'Aaron's right. That area's a marine sanctuary.'

Davey joined them. 'They could have been pirates Grandpa.'

The old man kept a solemn face. 'They could've been at that, young fella.'

'Can you catch them?'

'Not me. I'll tell the Coastwatch and they'll send a police boat round to check up on them.'

Ellie scowled. 'If they're killing wildlife I hope they go to gaol!'

Grandpa nodded. 'Oh if they're doing that, they'll go to gaol all right, *and* lose their boat.'

Davey beamed. 'The police'll take the bad men's boat?'

'That's right, impound it so they can't do it again.'

'Exc'lent,' pronounced Davey. 'Serve them right!' Grandpa marked something in the margin of his charts. Ellie knew he was hiding a smile but when he looked up again his face was quite serious.

'Keep your eyes skinned. I'll report this in the morning,' he said.

24

One afternoon a week later, they coasted down a sandy track to a small bay, with a tiny island about one hundred and fifty metres offshore.

'Isn't this Docker's Island — where we saw that fishing boat?' asked Ellie.

'It'd be too shallow in here for a boat that size,' said Aaron. 'They probably anchored in the channel closer to the island. That's still pretty sheltered.' He squinted across to its rocky outline. 'There's some incredible blue coral in this bay.'

Hot sun glared off the limestone rocks and the water sparkled clear and inviting. Ellie wiped the sweat from her face. 'Can we swim across?'

'At low tide we could wade out.' He glanced at Davey. 'But it's not low tide. What about you mate?'

Davey was already stripping off his shirt. 'I could swim right round that island easy, I bet.'

Aaron laughed, tossing aside his towel and reaching for his snorkeling gear. 'Just stick to the inside reef matey. Come on.'

Ellen had no doubts her brother could swim the distance. He was halfway to being a fish already. She made for the water, pulling on her own mask, while Nibs followed, splashing and barking at the circling gulls.

Nibs was what Aaron called a 'hairy dog-fish'. The border collie loved the water and paddled after them from reef to reef, resting on the highest ledges, swimming in circles above their heads when they dived.

With visibility up to four or five metres, Ellie followed the boys as they cruised in a half-circle towards the island. Ahead of her, Davey chased a small school of soldier fish, Nibs splashing furiously in his wake. Aaron swam back pointing to a whole rock covered in layers of vivid, iridescent blue.

Ellie nodded, her eyes wide in wonder. She paddled on, through waist-high water. Miniature blennies glared at her from holes in the pink coral. A pair of rainbow wrasse circled her feet and blended into purple weed. Clouds of golden bullseyes and midnight-blue pretty fins drifted in hollows under the reef. To Ellie it was a wonderland, more beautiful by far than any garden grown on land.

Suddenly she was aware of movement in the water, of Nibs barking and Davey shouting. She rose quickly and lifted her mask.

Around them a mob of seals slid and slipped through the water like silver shadows. One surfaced near Ellie, its eyes soft and cow-like, water dripping off its whiskers. Davey hooted with delight, but it was Nibs they'd come to play with. The dog splashed and turned, snapping and heaving himself at them as they leaped and dived over his head, driving him first one way, then the other. He was completely outclassed. All the way to the island they teased him. Then, just as suddenly, they vanished.

'Hey!' yelled Davey. 'Come back, you guys! Come back!' But the seals were gone and Nibs collapsed exhausted on the sandy beach, the children beside him.

'Wow!' gasped Ellie. 'Have you seen that before?'

Aaron's usual reserve deserted him. He shook his head. 'Wild,' he grinned. 'They sure had Nibs fooled.'

'Where'd they come from?' shouted Davey scanning the sea for signs.

'I'd guess they were fur seals that breed on beaches and offshore islands round here.' Aaron rolled his eyes. 'That was so epic!' He was almost lost for words. 'So wild.'

'Why Nibs?' asked Ellie.

'Why not Nibs,' demanded Davey who made no distinction between people and dogs.

'Perhaps they thought he was a sort of seal.'

'Whatever,' sighed Davey. 'That was the best, man. The best!' And he wriggled into the sand to warm himself.

Five minutes later he was calling Nibs, ready to explore Docker's Island. Aaron glanced up. 'Stick to the beach, Davey. Dugites breed in those rocks up there.'

'You heard, Davey Flannagan!' Ellie glared at him. 'Grandpa will kill me if you get bitten by a snake.'

He rolled his eyes at her, murmuring, 'Okay, o-kay.'

They wandered along the shoreline, Davey ever hopeful of finding his second leafy sea-dragon. Ellie kept an eye on him, muttering warnings about cone shells, sea-snakes and blue-ringed octopuses.

He frowned at her, insulted by her fussing.

Further up the beach, Nibs flushed out a pair of oystercatchers, chasing the big clumsy birds off the reef and up to the headland. 'Nibs!' yelled Davey. 'Here!' But the dog took no notice, tearing after the slow-moving catchers, barking delightedly. Davey raced after him.

Ellie started to call Davey back, Aaron's warning of snakes fresh in her mind. But she hesitated, unwilling to seem like a fusser again. Then it was too late. Davey was off up the rockface after Nibs. 'Davey!' she shouted. But he was gone.

'Jeez!' Aaron dropped his sack and belted after them.

Ellie rounded the headland a minute later to see Aaron halfway up the cliff. Nibs was at the top, growling and snapping at something on the rock. Davey was frozen where he stood. Aaron moved quickly in behind him. 'Don't move, little mate!' he murmured, trying to keep his voice calm. But Ellie could hear the fear in it. 'Leave Nibs. Back away!'

She crept closer. She could see the snake now. It was poised in a hollow on the cliff, head raised, hissing, ready to strike at Nibs.

'Oh God!' Ellie swallowed. She knew Davey would try to save Nibs, no matter what.

Aaron must have realised the same thing. He stood slowly, a large rock raised high above his head. 'Stay down, Davey!' he whispered. 'Don't move!' Then he hurled the rock, hard as he could, at the snake.

Everything happened at once then. The rock split into a hundred pieces, Ellie screamed. Davey grabbed Nibs. Aaron grabbed Davey, and the three of them half fell, half scrabbled their way back down to the beach, Nibs yelping and barking all the way.

Ellie was on her knees checking her little brother for broken limbs, snake-bite, anything. 'Jeez, Davey! You brain-dead little ...' She ran out of words. Davey, pale but determined, still had a firm grasp of Nibs' collar.

Aaron stood slowly. 'All okay, I think. The snake took off.' He examined the dog. 'Jeez we were lucky!'

Ellie swallowed and nodded. 'Thanks,' she murmured. 'That was really cool.' Davey buried his face in the dog's fur, mumbling his thanks, hiding his tears. Aaron shrugged, and nobody said anything else for at least three minutes.

It was a subdued little group that paddled slowly back to the mainland. There was no further sign of the seals, and when they stood shivering and drying themselves on the beach, Ellie said, 'We're going to have to teach that dog to obey, Davey. Or he can't come with us.'

Davey nodded. He squirmed into his parka. 'Starting tomorrow,' he said.

As they rode home a cold wind seemed to have sprung up from the south, and waves were moving steadily across the reef.

25

Davey was as good as his word. With advice from Mike Westway and Grandpa, he worked out a plan to spend at least an hour each day training Nibs.

That evening Ellie sat with Grandpa on the verandah.

'What's all this dog-training act?' quizzed Grandpa, peering over his glasses at Ellie. 'Why all of a sudden?'

Ellie shrugged. 'It's about time. He chased Mrs Westway's cat, and today he kept barking at a snake — wouldn't come away.'

Grandpa stared at her. 'A dugite?'

Ellie nodded.

'Where were you?'

'Just down the coast a bit.' She added guiltily, 'we could still see the lighthouse.'

'What happened?'

'Aaron scared it off.'

The old man watched her thoughtfully. 'You are being sensible, girl?'

She nodded, almost too quickly. 'Sure.'

'Anything else?'

Ellie shook her head. 'No,' she muttered.

He took off his glasses and cleaned them, flicking a sideways glance at her. 'Hmmph,' he said and went back to his shipping charts.

Ellie wriggled uneasily. She hadn't told Grandpa the whole story. Neither, she now realised, had Davey. It was a new thing for him. He usually blurted out his every adventure. Davey must be growing up, only telling adults what was safe for them to know. Ellie sighed. It's what she did herself at times, but it made her sort of sad.

The next day the weather turned cool. Wind howled and swooped around the cottage, driving big waves into Our Bay, swirling sand across the base of the cliff. Ellie found a safe spot out of the wind and curled up to watch the waves surge and pound onto the rocks below the lighthouse. This was her first real storm, and she loved the change in the sea's mood and colour. As she watched, a huge wave reared up and up, then up again, stretching its pale green glassiness to its highest point before curling over and crashing down in a mass of foam, stark white against grey clouds. Gulls and terns wheeled screaming across the darkening sky.

Ellie remembered Grandpa saying how wild and dangerous the sea could get. One part of her prayed that no one was caught in the storm out there, the other part revelled in the tossing wind and furious ocean. She wondered briefly about the boom in the dungeon, and secretly hoped she would feel the storm in the cottage that night.

She turned, hearing the Westway's Jeep pull into the yard. A few minutes later Aaron joined her. He leaned silently against the cliff, watching the flight of a tern through the drifting spray and churning water. A massive breaker hurled itself against the round walls of the lighthouse and Ellie felt the boom as it struck the rocks under her feet.

'Did you feel that?' she said. 'Grandpa says that in a really bad storm you can feel vibrations right through the house.'

'Is that because of the caves underneath?'

'I guess so.'

He gave a half-grin and shrugged himself away from the rock. 'I was hoping to see those caves — remember?'

Ellie nodded. 'Whenever,' she murmured.

Davey thundered round the corner. 'What're we doing?' he shouted, his voice blown away on the wind.

'Ellie's going to show me the dungeon,' said Aaron. 'You coming?'

Davey wasn't enthusiastic. 'It's all dark and slimy, and there are torture rings to chain up people.'

Ellie shivered. She was torn between agreeing with Davey and wanting to show Aaron the carving in the pit. Besides, the boom of the waves would be really major in the storm. She wanted to hear that boom, but the thought of the dungeon's damp coldness put her off. 'It really is quite spooky,' she murmured. 'We'll need a torch. You wouldn't want to be stuck down there.'

Aaron's eyes gleamed. 'Let's go,' he said.

They found a torch in the pantry and made their way outside. Wind whipped at their clothes and hair. Aaron heaved the trapdoor open and shone the light down into the darkness. A low continuous rumble echoed out of the pit and a cold dank smell gusted upwards. Ellie thought the whole place seemed even grimmer and more threatening than the first time. 'We're supposed to tell Grandpa where we are,' she murmured.

'I'll do it,' said Davey quickly. 'Nibs and me'll stay up here and tell Grandpa.'

Ellie pulled a face at him. 'Chicken!' she whispered, knowing she really didn't want to go into that black pit again either. But she followed Aaron down the ladder calling, 'Make sure that trapdoor stays open, Davey. And don't forget to tell Grandpa.' Her voice echoed back at her.

Inside, Aaron flashed the light around the cave.

'Grandpa's cleaning things,' explained Ellie, pointing to the pile in the corner.

'Yeah.' Aaron raised his head listening. 'Wow! Listen to that storm. That's the boom you were talking about?'

'Yeah.' She hoped she sounded cooler than she felt. The waves seemed to suck and crash just inches away — far louder than Ellie imagined it would be. She made herself reach out and touch the rock. 'You can feel it too,' she said.

Aaron put both hands against the wall. 'The whole cliff face must be a network of caves. Probably linked together, sending wave vibrations from one to another. I've felt the same thing diving in sea caves.' There was that eagerness in Aaron's voice again. Ellie was learning that when he had something he knew, or cared about, he sounded really different, and didn't mumble at all.

'Well, I just hope the sea doesn't break into this one,' she said. Ellie had to agree with Davey. The place was dark and spooky, like some monster's dungeon under the sea. It would be so bad to get trapped down here. She shivered as the thud and boom of the waves echoed around the cave. Well, she'd invited Aaron down to feel the wave vibrations and see the carving. She just hoped he didn't guess her shivers were as much for fear as for cold.

Ellie glanced irritably at the boy beside her. Now she thought about it, he'd almost asked himself down. And to top it off, he didn't seem to be worried in the slightest — or even think she might be. He was walking round, cool as you like, checking the vibrations in the rocks, peering into dark corners, checking levels of dampness in the floor. Ellie didn't like that dampness. It meant the sea was far too close on the other side of the rock wall. Almost snatching the torch from Aaron, she focused on the carvings. 'Over there,' she snapped and guided the torch beam downwards.

'Heh! Look at that!' whispered Aaron. He ran his hand over the marks, just as Ellie had done, then sat back on his heels. 'Sheez! *O.S.L. 1756*! How long's that before Australia became a British colony?'

Ellie forgot her irritation. 'Grandpa says about thirty-odd years earlier.' She wasn't sure who was the first European to land on Australian shores, but she did know 1756 was long before Captain Cook.

'You'd think someone would've done some research on it by now.'

'Grandpa's friend did go to Holland to check records, but nobody wanted to believe him. Besides, research costs money. If any of O.S.L.'s stuff turned up, stacks of people'd be interested.' She shrugged. 'Anyway, Grandpa says he doesn't want a whole bunch of eggheads down here.'

Aaron nodded. 'Dad's the same. They don't even want us to look any more. Well-ll,' he said, standing up slowly, 'that doesn't stop us. They're sure to have missed something. And we may get lucky — then they'd think differently.'

'As if,' Ellie laughed weakly, but she felt a thrill of excitement. She thought again of Larsen waiting for the ship that never came. If they found his cave, maybe some of his stuff would have survived. Then he wouldn't have just disappeared, unknown and unremembered. He'd be famous.

Aaron must have been having some of the same thoughts. He slid his hand over the initials again and shook his head. 'Poor dude. What a bummer ending up like that. He'd almost have been better drowning with the rest of his mates.'

Ellie shivered and murmured, 'I can't think why he'd hang around down here.'

Aaron stood thinking, then he frowned. 'But the guy carved his initials here, didn't he?'

'That's always assuming that Larsen *actually was* O.S.L. 1756 — and not a convict.'

Aaron ignored that possibility. 'So why'd he do that? Why here? Why waste his time?'

Ellie put Grandpa's case. 'What else had he got to do? Besides the Aborigines said Larsen carved all the time. Anyway there's no stuff here or anything.'

'Not now. Well okay. So this cave must've been checked a million times, but what about the others around it?'

Ellie shrugged. 'No point.' She winced at the sound of the waves so close by. 'Grandpa says the rest of the caves are usually below sea level. The waves wash in all the time. Nobody'd store stuff there.'

Aaron nodded. 'Yeah, I guess so.' The roar of the waves from the nearby caverns seemed to deepen, and he shivered too. 'Let's get out of here.'

26

Davey couldn't wait to show Aaron the rest of the house. 'There may be pirates one day,' he whispered.

As Ellie and Davey had done, Aaron crawled through the pirate hole in Ellie's wardrobe, explored the cellar and cupboards, and finished up staring at the door in Ellie's ceiling.

'Great house,' he sighed and shook his head. 'Must be epic to live here.' He pointed up. 'Where does that lead?'

'The roof,' announced Davey. 'Grandpa says there's a big space in the roof. It's all full of possum and rat shit, and old rubbish.'

'You'd have to say that wouldn't you?' Ellie glared at her brother and he shrugged.

She turned to Aaron. 'It's a big attic. You can only get there from a sort of ladder outside, near the chimney. Grandpa's going to fix it.'

'It'd be really neat to get up there,' said Aaron. 'There could be all sorts of stuff.' He gave a half-grin. 'Maybe I could fix those rungs. Would your grandpop mind?'

'I'll ask him this evening,' said Ellie. There had been no doubt in Ellie's mind that the attic must have been Mum's territory. Now she couldn't wait to get up there. She'd talk to him tonight.

That night over tea, Davey beat her to it. 'Can we get up into the roof Grandpa? Aaron says he'll fix the ladder. I'll help. I bet I could fix it too. Can we?'

The old man looked up from his Irish stew. 'What's the hurry?'

Ellie's cheeks were pink with excitement. She spoke without thinking. 'There may be some of Mum's stuff up there ...' Her voice trailed off. 'I mean ...'

Grandpa looked straight at her and nodded. 'I should have realised. You're right, lass. Mags often went up there.' He frowned. 'I don't think there's been anyone since.'

Ellie relaxed a little. Perhaps he hadn't been stalling. He'd probably just forgotten about Mum's stuff in the attic. 'Well we thought as it's stormy out, it might be a good time to see what's there.' She smiled winningly. 'And you did say we could go up.'

He read her thoughts. 'Don't hope for too much, girlie. Remember, it's not always wise to stir up old memories. Better to make new ones of your own.'

'It's cool, Grandpa,' said Ellie. 'I'm fine.'

'Yeah, Grandpa,' chimed in Davey. 'It's cool and we're fine.' He jiggled around excitedly. 'Haven't you ever been up there, Grandpa?'

'Not in thirty years, laddie,' he said, then sighed, ruffling Davey's hair. 'But you couldn't have kept me out at your age.' He glanced sideways at Ellie. 'Well I suppose it's as good a time as any — seeing as the storm's kept you CB.'

She was puzzled. 'Huh? CB?'

'Confined to Barracks — Stuck in the House — an old army term.'

'Oh. Okay, cool.' Ellie wondered, not for the first time, at the strange words adults used. 'Well,' she murmured, 'you did say you'd fix it — now Aaron will save you the trouble.'

'Fine.' Grandpa placed his knife and fork neatly in the centre of his plate. 'Spare rungs and tools are in the shed, but wait for a break in the weather.' He eyed Davey. 'And I don't want you on the roof until the ladder's fixed, young man.'

'Awwwwh.' Davey was outraged.

Grandpa ignored the pouting lip. 'You want to

162

get into the attic, you follow the rules.'

'But I was going to help Aaron.'

'I'll help Aaron, if he needs it.' He glanced at Ellie again. 'Just remember what I said. Sometimes memories hurt.'

The storm calmed a little the next day and now and then a watery sun glanced out of the banks of clouds. Aaron arrived early, ready to start on the ladder. In the end, the old man grumbled and hmmphed and gave him a hand with fixing the rungs. 'Then I'm off to check for storm damage,' he said. 'You can get the hatch open yourselves.'

By mid afternoon Ellie and Aaron were chipping away at the layers of white paint on the outside hatch that led into the ceiling space. Davey, forbidden to climb up until all was safe, hovered around below, asking every five minutes if they were finished yet.

Ellie was lost in her own thoughts. She imagined Mum up here, curled up with a book or a diary. Mum always kept one and there may be lots of diaries. Grandpa had said she was eighteen when she left home. Ellie wondered if she'd written about Michael Westway? Had they been sweethearts? Lovers? The word sounded odd to her mind. She wasn't exactly sure what it meant. She glanced quickly at Aaron, suddenly embarrassed. There were some things she didn't intend to share with anyone.

'Here she goes!' Aaron wrenched at the bolt and the small door swung outwards. He slid sideways and waited for Ellie to clamber through. Pale beams of light filtered in through a line of dusty skylights in the sloping roof. Cracks in the walls let in small bits of the day. The air was cold, slightly damp and musty. The loft shape followed what must have been half the kitchen, turning the corner to a dim space beyond: my bedroom, decided Ellie.

Davey, then Aaron squeezed up beside her. 'Wow,' breathed Davey scuttling across the floor, leaving tracks in the dust. He scratched at the caked glass in one of a row of peepholes along the outer wall. 'I can just see the lighthouse out there,' he shouted.

Ellie was more interested in what was inside. A pile of oars lay along one wall with some rotting canvas on top. A broken rocking horse and bits of several chairs were stacked in one corner, a trunk and other shapeless mounds in another. Grandpa was right about the possum dirt, it was everywhere.

Dust was inches thick. Ellie sneezed and smeared dirt across her face. They were going to have to clean up before they could spend time here.

She crouch-walked round the corner to the space above her bedroom. Beneath her feet she could make out the outline of a door. It was weird walking on her own ceiling. It didn't seem so dusty in here. At one end, a small alcove had been arranged with shelves and a chair. Ellie swallowed. There was only one person who could have done that.

Aaron appeared beside her. 'Find anything?'

She nodded towards the alcove, not looking at him. 'Over there.'

He stared at it for a minute. 'Your mum?'

'I guess so.'

He nodded. 'You'd better sort that out, then.' Ellie let her breath out. It was so simple. What was she worried about?

Aaron poked at a wooden trunk slowly disintegrating in another corner. A mouse scuttled out. He moved the trunk and others dashed across the floor. Ellie tried to muffle her 'Yeeuk!' She half stood, ready to leap out of the way.

Davey rushed round shouting. 'Action! Action!' The mice disappeared.

Aaron grinned. 'Only mice,' he murmured.

Ellie was furious with herself for squealing. 'Okay,' she snapped. 'So before anything, we need to clean the place out. I can hardly breathe.'

Davey started coughing. Aaron nodded. 'If it makes you feel better.' Ellie couldn't make up her mind if he was stirring or not.

Scrambling and hauling a reluctant Davey, they climbed down the ladder and into the kitchen. Ten minutes later they returned to the loft, equipped with buckets, rubbish bags, dustpans and everything else Ellie decided they might need.

An hour later the loft was a different place. Dust still floated in the air, but the room was swept and shovelled clean of mouldering dirt. Sunlight shafted through the scraped-off windows to make a strangely peaceful space. No one felt like talking.

Aaron worked at the catch of a trunk. Davey raced from peephole to peephole shooting pirates or aliens and other marauders. Ellie made her way to the alcove that she privately called 'Mum's corner'.

One of the mounds was an old leather case filled with books, folders and writing pads. Brushing off a cover, Ellie picked up one marked: *This book is the private property of Margaret Eleanor McCleod, Lighthouse Cottage, Larsen's Point, Australia, The World.* Ellie gasped, hugging the book to her and remembered a laughing Mum helping her fill out her own diary in almost the same way. The black pain flooded back and a deep sob started in her chest. She couldn't stop the tears. She hung her head, breathing deeply, trying to muffle her crying.

Grandpa had warned her the memories might hurt. Ellie just hadn't realised how much. She'd been fooling herself — sort of pretending that Mum wasn't dead. With each passing day, she'd pushed aside the real reason why Mum wasn't with them any more. The black wound inside her had been there, but patched over. Now it was raw and bleeding again. She huddled in her corner and gave in to the lost feeling and the misery.

After a while the sobs eased a little and she put the book down and tried to wipe her nose. She wished she had a pair of sunglasses or something to cover her red eyes. She glanced round at the others. Davey was burrowing through a box of strange-looking tools and Aaron had the trunk open examining its contents. Neither of them seemed to have noticed her tears.

Ellie took another deep breath, and worked her way through the rest of the things in the case. There were other diaries and some exercise books with stories and drawings in them. Mum had loved writing stories and poems. A pile of letters was tied with green ribbon, and a folder was marked, *Notes on O.S.L. 1756,* in strange writing, not Mum's.

Ellie needed to sit a moment and steady herself. The diaries she could read in her own time, that is if she could bear to read them at all. The letters — maybe she'd leave them too or wait until she was older. But the folder — they could all share the folder. She cleared her throat, hoping her voice didn't sound gulpy, as though she'd been crying. 'Hey you guys, found anything?'

'Ellie! Dungeon stuff!' Davey clanked at things in his box. 'These are weird tools, and look!' He rattled a piece of metal. 'Handcuffs!' They were too. Rusted and locked together, but undoubtedly handcuffs.

Aaron glanced over. 'Cool,' he murmured, 'What about a key?'

'There's about ...' Davey counted silently, 'six, yeah six keys, but they're all covered with yukky stuff.'

'We can get that off,' Aaron grinned. 'Might come in useful for keeping some little guys in line.'

The joke went over Davey's head. 'Yeah,' he breathed again. 'Pirates and guys like that.' He scuttled over and peered at Ellie. 'What's wrong with your face, Ellie?'

She ignored him and turned away. 'What about you Aaron?'

He shrugged, not looking at her. 'The trunk's full of maps and old charts and stuff. Some of it might be interesting. You find anything?'

She held up the folder. '*Notes on O.S.L. 1756,*' she read out.

'Okay! Neat!' He leaned over and took the folder. 'Hey! It's Dad's writing!' He flipped the pages. 'Why don't we take this down to the shed and look at it properly?'

'I like it here,' announced Davey, suspecting that once he left, he might not get back. 'I'll stay.'

Ellie shook her head. 'Uh-uh. C'mon Davey.'

He glared at her, the lip starting to show, then he frowned. 'You've been crying. Your face is all funny and your eyes are red.'

It was Ellie's turn to glare. She wished she could thump him one. If Aaron hadn't been there she would have. 'Hush up, Davey, just hush up!'

'But ...' he was worried now. 'Ellie don't cry. I ...'

'Come on you guys!' Aaron had moved off and was standing by the hatch. 'Bring those cuffs Davey and we'll get the rust off.'

Ellie brushed past her little brother, hugging him on the way. 'I'm okay,' she whispered. 'C'mon.'

Down in the shed, Ellie excused herself and went off to wash her face and clean up as best she could. When she came back, Davey beamed at her. 'You look nice,' he announced, not mentioning her face or eyes at all.

Aaron had his back to her and Ellie wondered if he'd been giving her small brother a lesson in tact. 'Okay,' she said. 'What've we got?'

Aaron had spread out a creased and grubby map. 'This landform map is Dad's. He's marked the places he and your mum looked. And this,' he slid a packet from its plastic sheath and unfolded it, 'is a copy of an old marine chart from the eighteenth century. It must be the one your grandpop's friend worked on. See, it's all marked with currents and likely search areas along the coast where wreckage, or a person, might be washed ashore.'

Ellie touched the maps reverently. 'These are so amazing — everything we need.'

'Yeah,' breathed Davey, ready to agree with anything.

'I haven't worked out why yet, it looks quite different from today's map of the area,' said Aaron, pointing to sections of the map. 'What we can do is transfer the information to a recent map. We can highlight all the searched areas in one colour and the possible areas in another. Dad's got stacks of coastline printouts at home we can use.'

28

Next morning Aaron spread his completed map on the kitchen table.

'You must have been going all night,' gasped Ellie. 'This is great! It's like that one your dad did for Mum.'

Aaron glanced at her quickly. 'He did one for her? Just like this?'

Ellie didn't know why she blushed. She muttered, 'More or less. The sea seems different. Shall I get it?'

'Just a minute.' He leaned over and pointed to the area around the lighthouse. 'Get this. I've been checking with Dad's recent maps, and it looks as if the tides are higher now than they were two hundred years ago.'

'What d'you mean?'

'See. The caves below the cottage and lighthouse are clearly marked in the old map. In the new maps, the entrances are all under water.'

'So Larsen's Cave is probably under water now?'

Aaron nodded. 'Could be. I read up about it. Some scientists now reckon that the world climate goes in an eleven year cycle, depending on these sun spots. If there's a really big spot, the weather freaks out and causes massive tides. Apparently Holland was nearly drowned about seventy years ago. At the other end of the cycle there'd be a massive freeze and the polar icecaps would expand and the sea level would fall.'

Ellie wrinkled her forehead. 'So what you're saying is that in Larsen's time there was a big freeze-up of the seas, and the dungeon and cold store could have been above water?'

'Looks like it — all up and down the coast — all over the world.' Aaron's eyes gleamed. Ellie could see he was really into this stuff. 'At the top of the cycle when these sun spots flared up, there'd be a heat wave. Then, like I said, parts of the polar icecaps would melt and the seas would rise and ...'

'... and cover parts of the land. We must be in the hot part now,' Ellie continued his reasoning.

'Right! Also in our time, there's global warming and stuff. The sea level has been rising, but in Larsen's time this part of the coast would have been a bit more exposed.'

Ellie could see where Aaron had coloured parts of the map to show where the sea level was once much lower. This included the section round the lighthouse and cottage. She remembered how there'd been shells in the middle of the desert out of Shelley. She told Aaron about the shells. 'The sea would have been hundreds of kilometres inland from where it is now. That'd be some massive meltdown of icecaps, eh?'

He shrugged. 'The Nullarbor was supposed to be a sea at one time, wasn't it? There'd be stacks of time the sea'd be higher than it is now. I guess there's probably other reasons these things happen too. It's a theory, anyway.'

'It makes sense, but doesn't do us any good, does it?' Something stirred in Ellie's memory. Somewhere she'd seen a place where there might be underwater caves. She couldn't put her finger on it and pushed the thought away. There was no point in worrying about drowned caves. She spoke her thoughts aloud. 'If you're right, we've got no hope of finding Larsen's Cave — if it is under water ...'

'What's under water?' Michael Westway limped in with Grandpa. 'And what's the map all about, son? As if I didn't know.'

Aaron shrugged at his dad. 'We found your notes

in the attic. We were just working out an idea.' He pulled a face. 'Nothing special.'

'And now you think you've got all the answers?'

Aaron shrugged again. Ellie came to his rescue. 'After we read your *Notes on O.S.L. 1756* folder, Mr Westway, we just added the places we've been. I mean,' she glanced at Grandpa. 'You knew all along we'd have to do a bit of looking.'

He glared at her, but she recognised the flicker in his eyes. He scowled. 'That stupid wild-goose chase. I wish I'd never mentioned it.' He shook his head. 'I suppose it's no use pointing out the number of people who've already tried to find this cave: me, the visiting expert, my mate, Mags, Michael here, and God knows who else.'

Ellie smiled weakly and wriggled. Davey threw his arms round Grandpa's legs. 'Don't be cross Grandpa,' he pleaded.

Aaron's dad said, 'I guess you'll never believe we could do as good a job as you.'

Aaron shrugged. 'It's not that, Dad. We might just get lucky. And you didn't have the diving gear we have now.'

That was a mistake. Hamish McCleod stood up frowning. 'Ellie and Davey are not to dive in any cave,' he growled. 'And you should know better. I don't want to start confining you to barracks, but …'

Aaron went red in the face and scuffed the floor. 'Yeah, I know Mr McCleod, I …'

His dad chimed in, 'I want your promise Aaron — underwater caves are out of bounds.'

'Yeah, sure Dad,' Aaron sighed, rolling his eyes at Ellie. 'Look. No sweat! We're only doing what you guys did. Why's everyone getting so heavy?'

Ellie knew Grandpa was worried for them. 'It's okay, Grandpa. We'll be sensible.'

He glared at her and snorted, 'I'm holding you to your promise.'

Ellie nodded. 'Cool.' She nudged Davey.

'Yeah,' he shouted. 'Cool! Me too.'

29

The storm blew itself out and the dark clouds turned to swirly white mare's tails in a scrubbed blue sky. Feeling a bit guilty about Grandpa, Ellie offered to check out the wildlife sanctuary to see if there were any storm casualties or bad washaways.

He glared at her. 'I know you're softening me up, girlie. Your mother used to do the same.' Despite the glare, Ellie could hear amusement rather than anger in his voice. He added gruffly, 'I'd be grateful if you'd check out the East Sanctuary — but no exploring. Stay clear of cliff faces and overhangs. Storm damage can undermine limestone cliffs.'

'Okay. No worries.'

A short while later Aaron joined Ellie and Davey and they set off on their bikes. The sea was still choppy with a big swell running. A strong southerly wind battered at them as they pushed steadily on, checking each cove and bay as they came to it. Clouds tumbled about the sky and most beaches were covered in banks of weed and sea rubbish. In many places the sand had been scoured away, exposing the rocks underneath.

Davey, with Nibs in tow, raced the wind round corners and down hills, whizzing through the sanctuary gates, whooping and shouting like a wild Indian. Suddenly he skidded to a halt, dropped his bike and ran, crouching, back up the track to Aaron and Ellie. 'They're there again!' he hissed. 'Those crooks in the boat. They're on the beach.'

Ellie and Aaron left their bikes and joined Davey and Nibs to wriggle forward on their stomachs to the edge of the cliff. A dinghy bobbed about on the calmer inner waters of the bay. Two men squatted on the beach cleaning fish. Further out, still sheltered from the weather by the arms of the cliffs, the *Atlantis 3* rode at anchor.

Aaron scowled. 'You're right Davey. It's the same nerdos. They're not supposed to be here.'

Ellie hunched her shoulders. 'Maybe they had to shelter from the storm.'

'And dump all their garbage on the beach?' Cans, soggy cigarette packets and plastic cartons drifted along the shoreline, orange peel and stale vegetables lay scattered about. Clouds of gulls wheeled and dived for the fish guts on the sand.

'Yuk!' Ellie wrinkled her nose. 'Morons! I bet they're going to leave all that mess there.'

Aaron swore under his breath and asked, 'Did you tell your grandpop before?'

Ellie nodded. 'He said you were right. They shouldn't be here and he reported them.'

Aaron growled again. 'Yeah well, they're still here. I bet they're taking fish — all sorts of stuff they're not meant to.' He shaded his eyes from the sun. 'What's that black thing further up? It looks like a seal. Maybe it's injured.'

Davey squinted hard. 'Hey! Yeah! It is a seal. A baby seal.' He frowned in concentration. 'It looks sick. Can we go see it, can we?' He half-rose and Nibs started barking.

A bald man with a thick, matted beard stood wiping his hands on the back of his jeans. The other in a check shirt yelled something, but the wind took it away. It didn't sound friendly.

Nibs scampered down the cliff on to the beach, Davey after him. Ellie's call went unheeded. Aaron was already on his way.

As they reached the beach, the man with the beard

stepped forward snarling, 'Hey you kids! What'dya want? Push off — go home!'

Davey raced past his outstretched arms. Ellie heard the man swear then grab at Davey, but the small boy wriggled out of his grasp, shouting, 'Rack off Hairy-face!' and went after Nibs.

The check-shirted man turned scowling at Aaron. 'Listen mate! Get out of here now! Before you and that smart-tongued brat get hurt.'

Aaron stood his ground, Ellie beside him. 'You're not meant to be here,' he said. 'This is a marine park.'

Hairy-face breathed heavily and snorted, 'So what? We're sheltering from the storm and it's none of your business. Now bugger off!'

Nibs had stopped to nose at three large, bulging bags. Check-shirt kicked him hard, sending him yelping and tumbling into a weed bank.

Davey didn't hesitate. He launched himself at the man's legs, catching him off balance and sending them both crashing into the water. Nibs was back to help in a minute, growling and tugging at the man's shirt.

As Hairy-face grappled with Aaron, Ellie ducked past and rushed to Davey's rescue. She untangled the dripping boy from the mess of legs, sand and snapping Nibs. The man struggled to his feet, swearing and reaching out to grab Davey. Ellie pushed herself in front of her brother. 'Morons!' she shouted. 'Go away. I'll tell my Grandpa! Filthy, rubbish-dumping morons!'

A taller man in a battered captain's cap appeared from under the lee of the cliff, hands outstretched, voice soothing. 'Hey, hey! Kids! No harm, heh? Everyone get too mad. Now we talk, nice and sweet, heh?'

Davey took his chance and broke away, racing up the beach to check out the seal. Aaron was losing his struggle with Hairy-face. Ellie stood panting, shaking sand from her face and hair. She was so mad she had to force herself to calm down. She gritted her teeth and ground out, 'This is a wildlife sanctuary. You are not allowed to hunt, *or* —' she pointed at the gutted fish, 'fish here. My grandpa is the Ranger. He'll report you.'

A dripping wet Check-shirt swore, jerked his finger in the air and stomped off. He was back a minute later shouting at them to 'Get lost', and wringing salt water from his shirt tail.

Ellie boiled inside. These were the scumbags who dumped on beaches and damaged wildlife. She felt like shouting every swear-word she knew at them.

But it wasn't natural for her to be rude, so she hesitated, waiting red-faced and eyes glaring, to hear what the leader had to say.

'Heh, leetle lady,' he cooed, smiling over tobacco-stained teeth. 'Why you so mad? We poor feeshermen sheltering from storm. We need food — we catch feesh to eat.' He raised his shoulders. 'We go soon. We no cause trouble.'

'What about all the rubbish?'

The captain shook his head and flicked a shoulder at his mates. 'They peasants. Know nothing. I make them clean up.'

Ellie was running out of things to say. She glanced at the bulging sacks on the beach. 'What's in those?' she asked.

He shrugged. 'Nothing important — feesh, some supplies from the boat ... nothing important.'

Ellie didn't believe him. She moved towards the bags, but at a look from his leader, Hairy-face let go of Aaron and stepped in front of her, holding her arm, fending her off.

30

Just then there was a long, 'No-o-o-o-o!' from the other end of the beach. Ellie struggled to join her brother, but Hairy-face still held her. Aaron raced after Davey, dragging him back down the beach, away from the seal. As they got closer, Ellie could see the little boy was in tears. Aaron looked pale-faced, almost sick.

'The seal's had its throat cut,' he muttered. 'It's a pup and they've cut its throat.'

Check-shirt swiped his finger across his throat and laughed. 'Cut, cut, cut,' he sniggered.

Davey ran screaming and banging his fists against the man. 'Murderer!' he yelled. 'Scumbag murderer! They're gunna put you in gaol! My Grandpa'll tell and they'll take your boat away! Scumbag murderers!'

The man grabbed him and held him at arm's length by the scruff of his collar. Hairy-face let go of Ellie to watch, laughing and yelling advice to his friend.

The captain stepped in, hands pushing down in a calming action. 'Heh-heh-heh leetle man. Not so mad. Its momma die in storm. We have to put it out of its misery. Was only theeng to do.'

It was, Ellie knew, perfectly possible. The mother could have been hurt in the storm. It could have happened that way. Grandpa had to do the same sometimes. No one could prove these men were lying. Still all her instincts told her something was badly wrong. The only thing was to grab Davey and report back to Grandpa as soon as they could.

Davey was bent on his own solution. Nothing was going to convince him that the baby seal had to die. He shoved against his captor's hand, fists swinging wildly, feet kicking out. 'Scumbags!' he screamed again. 'Bloody nerdos!'

Nibs attached himself to the leg of the man's jeans, snarling and jerking his head from side to side. Aaron tried to free Davey but a fist knocked him sideways. Check-shirt turned to laugh and one of Davey's kicks caught him in the shin. The man swung and his blow glanced off the small boy's head. 'Little rat!' he screamed, his face red with rage, 'I'll get you. You're dead!'

Aaron sprang up, shouldered the man out of the way and shoved a dazed Davey behind his back. 'Ratshit!' he hissed. 'Bully! Clean up your bloody mess and get out of here.'

Snarling, Check-shirt made ready to throw a punch. The captain put a hand on his arm. 'Hey, hey. Leave this leetle rat to me.' He shoved Aaron aside, reaching for Davey. 'Thees little rat's gonna get a good hiding.' He raised his hand and Nibs went berserk, sinking his teeth into the man's leg, growling like a lion.

The man kicked and hit out at the dog, trying to shake Nibs from his leg. 'I'll keell this mutt!' He reached for his fishing knife. 'Bloody meddling keeds, I keell your dog!'

'Don't you touch him, scumbag!' shouted Davey — white in the face and grabbing for Nibs. 'Don't you bloody touch him!'

The captain's smile had vanished. There was no suggestion of any 'nice and sweet talk' now. 'Rotten leetle brat! Leave!' he snarled. 'Leave! Now! Get out! Go — or you get hurt. No more meddling. No more dog. No more keeds!'

Hairy-face and Check-shirt closed in to help their

leader and Ellie was left alone. She glanced quickly at the sacks. There had to be something bad in them, some evidence that would send these morons to gaol. She slid down and ripped them open — and was nearly sick. Piles of sleek dark skins, stained with blood, spilled out on to the sand. Sealskins! At least fifty sealskins! She couldn't bring herself to look in the other sacks. She swallowed back the rising vomit, but a cry of horror tore from her throat. 'Oh God! ... No!'

Everyone stopped. Nibs let go his victim and raced to her side, licking her face, rubbing his body against hers. Ellie was sick to her stomach — frozen. Piles of empty dead furs lay on the beach — furs that had once been beautiful sleek animals leaping and slipping through the sea like they had on that day at Docker's Island. She looked at the captain, her eyes wide with hatred and disgust. 'You *are* murderers!' she whispered, her voice cracking. 'Killers! You'll go to gaol for ever and ever for this!'

The captain stepped forward, face hard, all oiliness gone from his voice. His grin was ugly, full of menace. 'Very stupid, leetle missy — very stupid. Sacks not your business.' He started to move towards her.

For the first time Ellie felt fear. Sweat broke out on her hands and her stomach contracted. The sealskins were hard evidence and the captain knew it. If Grandpa told the coastguard, these men *would* go to gaol. They *would* lose their boat — everything. They couldn't let that happen. They'd never let her escape to tell Grandpa. She got to her feet. The man kept moving towards her, pulling a strong white rope from his pocket. 'I think you come with me now,' he said.

Nibs sensed the increasing danger and went into attack stance. From a bouncing, larrikin pup he became a copy of his wild forebears. Teeth bared, fur rising, he seemed to grow twice his size. And the growl, from deep within his throat, held all the threat of an ancient wolfpack. The captain hesitated. In that moment Aaron yelled, 'Run Ellie! Run! Get out of there. Come on!'

She responded instinctively, diving through the gap between the other two men to join the boys already sprinting back up the sandhills. Nibs raced at her heels whirling every now and then to bark and snarl a warning at anyone who threatened his humans.

The captain snapped an order, but the other men were off their guard, too caught up in events to stop the children's break for freedom. Hairy-face followed, panting and stumbling after Ellie. His flailing hands tore at her windcheater, lost their grip and dropped away. She raced on, struggling through the soft dunes, aware of heavy breathing and thumping sand behind her.

At the top of the last sandhill Aaron stood waiting. He pulled Ellie past him and shoved Check-shirt into Hairy-face so that they both rolled backwards down the shifting dune face.

Davey had already mounted as Ellie and Aaron swung on to their bikes. They pedalled furiously along the track. Back to his old self, Nibs bounced along beside them. Glancing back, Ellie saw the two men stagger into view on top of the dunes. They paused there a moment, waving fists and shouting words that were lost in the distance.

As the shouts faded, Davey skidded to a halt and leaped off his bike, whooping and jeering. 'Sucked in!' he shouted and quick as a flash whipped down his pants and wriggled his bare backside at the figures on the horizon. 'Sucked in!' he shouted again. 'Sucked in y'morons!' Ellie didn't bother to object. Neither did Aaron. 'C'mon mate,' he muttered. 'We're not home yet.'

Davey grinned, pulled up his pants and zoomed off on his trusty bike. Riding slower now Aaron turned to Ellie. 'What was in the bags?'

She swallowed, feeling sick again. 'Sealskins! Stacks of sealskins — all bloody and everything.'

She forced the vomit down, taking deep breaths.

He scowled. 'I suspected as much. That baby seal was scarred or its pelt would have been in the bag with the rest.'

Ellie shuddered. 'How can anyone do such a thing?'

'Money!' Aaron kicked at the ground in disgust. Then he looked sideways at her. 'I don't think it's over yet, do you?'

'What d'you mean?' She wasn't sure she wanted to hear the answer.

'Well, they're sure to know the Ranger Station is at the lighthouse, *and* they know we're going to report them, so ...' he shrugged. 'They've either got to dump the evidence and hide *Atlantis 3* from the Coastwatch — which won't be easy if the police bring in spotter planes — or they've got to stop us sounding the alert.'

Ellie's lips felt numb. 'How?' she whispered.

Aaron looked her straight in the eye. 'How do you think?' Even as he spoke an outboard engine roared into life in the distant bay, the sound coming closer and closer as the dinghy moved their way.

'Grandpa,' croaked Ellie. 'They'll get to Grandpa before we can.'

'C'mon,' snapped Aaron. 'We've got to warn him.'

31

The track was bumpier, the distance longer than ever Ellie remembered. It was taking far too much time to get back to Grandpa. Her legs felt rubbery and weak, the bike heavy and clumsy. Every now and then she caught the sound of the outboard motor. 'We won't make it, will we?' she panted, pushing her bike through the thick sand.

Aaron grunted something and pushed on. A few minutes later they reached the spot where a track led to Aaron's house. He was waiting there for Ellie, Davey was still ahead.

'They've got to take the boat out to sea to get through the break in Straggler's Reef. That'll slow them down a bit, but they're still travelling ten times faster than we can.'

Ellie gripped the handlebars tightly. 'What will we do?'

'It's no use racing back if they're there already and waiting for us. But we have to at least try and warn your grandpop. That doesn't need all of us. You and Davey take off here and go to my place. You'll be safe there.' Aaron put two fingers in his mouth and whistled Davey back.

Ellie frowned. There was no way she could abandon Grandpa to those men. After all she'd stirred the whole business up in the first place. 'I'm going to the Lighthouse. Davey knows the back way to your place. He'll be okay on his own. If they catch one of us, the other can still get help and we've got more chance of helping Grandpa. There're three men, remember.'

Aaron shook his head. 'Look they're not fooling around. Those nerdos are dangerous. You're a girl … girls can't …'

'Girls can!' snapped Ellie. 'I'm coming.'

In the distance the dinghy motor revved and swung closer. Aaron glanced out to sea. 'Listen, you could be hurt and we haven't time to get into this.'

Ellie nodded sharply. 'Right! So let's get moving. It's *my* grandpop and I'm coming.' Aaron scowled again but there was no time to argue.

Davey zoomed back, his cheeks flushed with the excitement. 'What're we doing?'

Aaron squatted down to speak to him. 'Listen mate, those nerdos are in that dinghy out there. They know we're from the lighthouse. They're heading there now. They might get there before us. You've got to go and get help.'

Davey nodded eagerly, his eyes shining. The adventure was getting better and better. 'I'll ride to Larsen's, I'll get the police, I'll get Grandpa!'

'No matey — *they* might get Grandpa. That's the problem.'

Davey's eyes widened. 'Grandpa?' he whispered, suddenly doubtful.

'Yes.' Aaron held his gaze. 'We've worked this out. And here's what you have to do. You know how this track goes round past the lighthouse to my place?'

Davey nodded vigorously. 'Sure, I been that way heaps of times.'

'Right. You shoot off this way and get help from Dad. Okay?'

Davey nodded. 'Sure ... But ...' he wriggled uncomfortably. 'Your mum doesn't like me, or Nibs,' he whispered.

Aaron frowned. 'That's nothing. Get to Dad. Tell him there are bad men trying to hurt your grandpop. Tell him we've gone to warn him. Now go!'

Davey hesitated, looking at Ellie.

'Go, Davey,' she whispered. 'Get help. We'll help Grandpa.' And the little boy nodded quickly, then raced off, Nibs in hot pursuit.

Aaron was already on his bike. 'Well c'mon,' he muttered. 'We'll be able to see if they're there when we get to the last hill.'

Ellie nodded. She was scared but there was no way she could leave Grandpa to face those men alone, and the thought of them anywhere near her beloved Lighthouse Cottage made her feel sick. She followed Aaron, pedalling furiously towards the final hill and whatever waited for them on the cliffs below.

32

Cresting the hill above the cottage, Aaron and Ellie flung themselves from their bikes. Lying on their stomachs they shaded their eyes against the evening sun. Almost at the same moment the dinghy rounded the headland and roared into Our Bay. There seemed to be only two men in it — the captain and Check-shirt.

'They've left Hairy-face behind,' whispered Aaron. 'One less scumbag for us to worry about.'

Ellie swallowed. She wasn't sure how they could deal with even two of them. 'There's Grandpa,' she muttered pointing. Grandpa was making his way towards the dungeon, loaded down with cleaning gear. He had obviously finished work for the day. He dropped the stuff on the ground and walked towards the beach as the incoming dinghy cut its motor and slid into the shallows.

Ellie half-rose, the warning cry dying on her lips as Aaron pulled her back down. 'Shush dummy! The crooks will hear you and get us too.'

'But what'll we do? Grandpa won't have a clue something's wrong.'

'Maybe not, but he'll be careful.' Aaron turned and faced Ellie. 'We can't reach him before they do, so we're going to have to wait our chance. They'll probably start off saying they're storm-damaged or something. While they're talking we'll have to sneak in and try and warn him.'

Ellie nodded. 'Okay but shouldn't we call the police or someone? There's a phone inside the lighthouse as well as the cottage.' She peered at the white cone soaring into the blue sky. It looked so solid and safe. If only they could reach it.

Beside her, Aaron pointed to the old-fashioned telephone lines running into the buildings. 'They'll work that one out too. We'll have to move fast before they cut the lines.' He screwed up his eyes against the glare. 'The door's shut. Is it locked?'

Ellie nodded miserably. 'Probably, and the key's in the kitchen, by the door — or in Grandpa's pocket.'

'So okay then. We need the key. You know the place better than I do. Go by the chook-run and into the cottage. I'll hang out by the lighthouse and stuff up their dinghy if I get the chance. Then at least they'll be stuck here.'

By now Grandpa had met the men who were waving their arms about and talking wildly.

Ellie slid down the side of the hill and at a crouching run took off for the rear of the cottage. She reached the back door easily enough and slipped into the kitchen. Through the window she glimpsed Grandpa listening to the two men as they walked towards the cottage. She glanced up at the rack. No lighthouse key — Grandpa must have it in his pocket.

Suddenly voices were sounding close to the kitchen door. They were coming inside. Sweat broke out on Ellie's hands. She slid into the pantry, pulling the door half-closed behind her.

The men came in, Grandpa ahead of the others. 'If you've an injured crewman,' he was saying, 'I'll ring for an ambulance to meet us here.'

'No, no meester Ranger,' Ellie recognised the captain's voice. 'Is not necessary. I geeve first-aid. You come and help ship off reef.'

She peeked out through the gap in the door frame. Grandpa was standing with arms crossed over his chest, eyeing the two men suspiciously. 'You say seven kilometres east of here? That's in the marine sanctuary. What were you doing there?'

'We shelter from storm. Our ship damaged. You Ranger, you come to help.'

The old man shook his head. 'I'll notify the authorities first. We may need help from Coastwatch. I'll tell them to stand by.' He moved towards the telephone on the wall.

'No!' The captain moved to intercept him. 'You come. Now!'

Grandpa narrowed his eyes. 'Move away please. I'm going to ring the Coastwatch.'

'Not to move!' The captain barked out the order. Ellie stifled a gasp. He had a knife out, pointed at Grandpa. 'You do as I say!'

There was a long moment of silence. Ellie saw Grandpa glare at the intruders. 'Damn you!' he hissed. 'Get out of the way! This is my lighthouse and my Ranger Station. I give the orders here!' He moved again towards the phone.

'We have cheeldren!' The words echoed round the kitchen.

Grandpa stiffened and faced the captain. 'You have what?' he ground out.

Check-shirt laughed. 'We have your stupid kids, old man — and their stupid dog. They're dead.'

The captain snapped at Check-shirt to shut up and

turned to the old man. 'Not dead — we just squeeze them leetle bit.'

Grandpa had gone pale. His eyes glittered. 'Don't you lay one bloody finger on them,' he grated. 'Not one bloody finger!'

Ellie wanted to shout, 'They're lying, Grandpa! We're here!' But she waited silently behind the pantry door, forcing herself to keep perfectly still, to breathe quietly.

It was important to keep calm. The men were trying to trap Grandpa into going with them. Then he'd be their prisoner and unable to raise the alarm. She tried to think of what to do. Glancing into the kitchen, she saw both the captain's and Check-shirt's backs were to her. Quickly she slipped out of her hiding place into Grandpa's line of vision, then back again. He blinked fast and looked down — but he'd seen her! She knew he'd seen her! She wasn't sure if that'd done any good, but at least he wouldn't worry now. She heard him clear his throat.

'Okay. So you have my children. Take me to them.' He flipped a key out of his pocket and hung it casually on the rack, then turned to his captors. 'Get on with it then!'

Check-shirt sniggered and flung open the kichen

door. 'Out you go Grandpop,' he sneered. 'Now *you* do what *we* say!'

Grandpa snorted, muttered something under his breath, and strode out of the kitchen. The captain went to follow, then turned and ripped the telephone off the wall. He seemed to hesitate, then called to Check-shirt. When the man returned, they went into a huddle, pointing and glancing up to where the track was. Ellie swallowed. They were talking about them. Well, at least Davey was safe, and Aaron was hiding — wasn't he?

Check-shirt went outside and called to someone. The answer made Ellie's stomach turn over. Hairy-face! How had he got here? He wasn't supposed to be here! He must have been hiding, waiting to trap them. God! Had something happened to Aaron? Surely she'd have heard something? If they did know she and Aaron were here, they could make Grandpa do whatever they wanted.

Someone was searching the back garden, banging cray pots, stirring up the chooks. Steps sounded on the side verandah. Ellie pressed herself against the wall. The captain shouted an order; Hairy-face grunted a reply. A shadow moved across the kitchen windows. God! He was right outside the kitchen door! She froze. They'd try the house next and find the pantry in no time. She could hide in the cold store, but that was easy to find too. What should she do?

There was a shout outside and she heard Grandpa yell, 'What are you waiting for? Maybe you don't have my kids after all.' The men turned towards him and in that instant Ellie slipped out and scuttled down the passageway to her bedroom. There was *one* place they'd never find her — the pirate hole!

Hairy-face stayed to search the house. For what seemed like hours he clumped around the cottage, shifting furniture, banging cupboards. Then he was in her room, muttering and swearing under his breath, pulling her bed aside, flinging open the wardrobe.

Behind the secret door Ellie went rigid. Her heart thumped so loud she thought he must hear. She almost stopped breathing, and the thought of his fat hands shoving her clothes around nearly made her sick.

She crouched there listening to him panting only inches from her face. She closed her eyes. God! Don't let him find the catch that moved the hidden door! The seconds seemed like hours, then the searching sounds faded and he was gone. A moment later the kitchen door banged and the men's voices moved away.

Slowly, Ellie let out her breath. It wasn't over by a long shot but they'd missed her this time. She slipped into the kitchen and grabbed the big brass lighthouse key from where Grandpa had deliberately replaced it on the hook. He knew she'd work out what to do.

She peered out. Check-shirt had Grandpa in an arm lock. They had all crossed the yard and were moving down the slope towards Our Beach. There was no sign of Aaron. Thank God! He must be okay. Ellie didn't hesitate. Slipping outside into the gathering dusk, she skittered across the grass to the lighthouse door. 'Aaron!' she hissed, struggling to fit the big key into the lock, 'Aaron they've got Grandpa. Where are you?'

There was no answer. She tried not to worry. With any luck, Aaron was on his way back from the beach; better still, he'd stuffed up the dinghy so the seal killers couldn't take Grandpa anywhere.

She glanced at her watch, the big beam was due to begin any minute. Her stomach turned over. The light might draw the captain's attention to the lighthouse. He might work out about the second phone. There was no time to lose!

Ellie swallowed, forcing hands and breathing to slow down. It'd be dumb to panic. The plan was all working out. All she had to do was stay cool.

The door swung open and she was inside.

The phone was on the wall by the door. In the semi-darkness, Ellie felt rather than saw, the zero. 000! It *was* 000, wasn't it? ... The emergency number *was* 000? Suddenly she was unsure — maybe that was on the telly for somewhere else. She tried it ... then again — 000.

A voice crackled over the line. 'Police? Fire? or Ambulance?'

'Police,' squeaked Ellie.

'Name please, and location.'

'Ell ...' she began. Then a hand covered her mouth, stifling the words. A large, hairy arm reached over her head. The telephone was torn out.

'Gotcha Sweetheart,' purred Hairy-face. 'No phone calls today!'

At that moment a low hummmm started up, and the lighthouse beam sprang out across the darkening sea. From the doorway Ellie heard the captain's voice, 'Now Meester Keeper! We do really have both your cheeldren!'

Her heart sank. They must have caught Aaron too.

33

Hairy-face frog-marched Ellie outside. Overhead, the big light flashed its cheerful warning to ships at sea. She took a wavering breath. Things did not look so cheerful here.

On the grass, only a few feet away, his face twisted in pain, was Aaron. They must think he was her brother. She had a sudden memory of him in the shed saying they were 'sort of related' — not that it made any difference now. Check-shirt had Aaron's head in a throat-lock, arms twisted behind his back.

'What happened?' gasped Ellie.

Aaron answered through tight lips. 'Hairy-face must have been lying in the boat, or hiding. Anyway, we missed him. Then he,' he flicked his head at Check-shirt, 'he came out and caught me. They were looking for us.'

Ellie nodded. 'Yeah I hid …'

Hairy-face wrenched her wrist and shouted, 'Put a sock in it you kids. No talking!'

Grandpa stood rigid with rage but just as helpless as Ellie. 'Let her go!' he hissed. 'You've got me! Don't touch her, you animal.' Hairy-face grinned and twisted Ellie's arm higher. She bit back a scream.

'Let her go!' roared Grandpa again. The captain barked an order and the man loosened his grip slightly.

'Now pleeeese,' the leader turned to Grandpa, hands outstretched. 'We don't want to hurt anybody. But,' he shrugged, 'my men angry. Thees boy break boat. We must get back to our ship.' He glanced round the yard. 'Where is small boy and dog?'

No one answered.

'Where?' snapped the captain and muttered something to Check-shirt who tightened his necklock on Aaron.

'Tell him, Ellie,' muttered Grandpa.

She swallowed, looked the man straight in the eye and lied, 'He went home to his mum ages ago. He doesn't even know you're here. Anyway,' she shrugged, 'he was feeling sick.'

The captain stared at her for a moment. Then he shrugged. 'No matter we go now. We take truck and go!' He put his hand out to Grandpa. 'Keys, old man!' he demanded. 'Keys!'

In the flashing light and shadows, the old man stood at bay like a fierce and ancient lion, but he couldn't do anything. 'On the kitchen peg!' he shouted. 'Take the bloody ute and get out! And don't ever come back.' Check-shirt sniggered and pretended to shake in fear.

The captain suddenly pointed at the trapdoor to the dungeon.

Hairy-face wrenched open the hatch. 'Ahh — a cellar, Captain — a nice dark cellar with a bolt we can pull across.'

The captain moved closer to Ellie and smiled horribly. She could smell the sour tobacco on his breath. 'There,' he sneered. 'You all go down there. Thees time we make sure you don't escape — not for a long, long time.' He pointed again. 'Now! All of you — down there!'

Grandpa scowled. 'You can't lock these children up down there. It's cold and damp. There's no light.' The captain gave a short laugh and flicked his head at his two henchmen. They shoved their prisoners forward.

Aaron only just stopped himself from falling head first down the steep stairs. Ellie followed, her hands slipping on the slimy rock walls. She tried to ignore the dank seaweed smell that surged up from the darkness below — and the thumping echo of the waves. Above her she heard Grandpa yell. Something large and heavy blocked the light, then the old man's body came tumbling and slithering down the steep stone steps.

'Grandpa!' Ellie's scream echoed in the darkness. Her lips were tight with fear. No sound came from the body at her feet. Terror made her rigid. They'd killed Grandpa! He was dead. She had lost him too!

Her shaking hands found his face. She felt desperately for his breathing — for any sign of life. Something wet and sticky came away on her fingers. In the dim light she glimpsed blood ... then the trapdoor slammed shut and the bolt crashed home. There was the muffled sound of something heavy being dragged across the hatch — then silence! Silence and blackness. Ellie could hardly breathe. They were trapped! Buried alive in the dungeon with the sea rising only metres away! Her nightmare had come true. It was even worse — Grandpa was dead!

34

Waves of shock shuddered through Ellie's body. She pulled the old man's head into her lap and struggled to shut out the horror that filled her mind.

Aaron crawled up beside her, his hands feeling for the old man's pulse. 'He's alive,' he whispered. 'His pulse is not too bad. He's going to be okay.'

Ellie didn't believe him, didn't really hear him. She'd lost Mum. Now she was losing Grandpa! The breath gathered in a tight ball in her chest. He was dead — or he was going to die! She screamed again. 'Grandpa! Noooooo!'

'He'll be okay!' She felt Aaron's hands on her shoulders shaking her. 'Ellie! He's going to be all right!'

Ellie sobbed mindlessly, not believing, letting the black pain engulf her. 'Grandpa,' she whimpered. 'Grandpa, Grandpa, Grandpa ...'

Aaron's arms reached round her, hugging her. 'He's not going to die Ellie. He's hurt a little bit. He'll be okay. Shhhshhh ...' he rocked her gently and held her until the sobs faded. 'Here's his hand. See, it's warm, it's alive!' He folded her fingers around Grandpa's large, rough hand. 'Hold his hand. He'll wake up soon.'

Ellie held tight, fighting the cloud of fear and misery that waited to roll through her head — through her whole body. She sensed Aaron beside her. It was too dark to see his face, to see Grandpa's face either. She tried to make her breathing normal, to smother the sobs that kept welling up inside her throat.

On the other side of the dungeon, the sea murmured and rumbled against the cave wall, echoing the shudders in Ellie's mind. The sea, the sea — always the sea. She wished it would stop pushing itself into her head, taking over her brain.

Suddenly she felt a movement under her fingers. Grandpa's hand moved in hers and he muttered something. He was alive! 'Grandpa!' she whispered, hope flooding into her voice 'Grandpa! I'm here. I'm here! You're alive! Do you hurt?'

He mumbled again. Ellie bent her ear to his lips. She could feel his breath on her cheek. The old man's voice croaked out of the darkness. 'I'll live girlie. I'll live!' He struggled to pull himself up. She heard him grunt in pain.

There was another grunt of pain as Aaron hauled him into a sitting position against the bottom step.

'Better rest, sir,' muttered the boy, wiping his hand. 'Shouldn't move too much. I think you're bleeding at the back of your head.'

'Buggers clobbered me one … in the head — and the ribs.' He gasped for breath. 'Something's gone in my ankle too.' He coughed and winced, 'Aaah! And *that* was a rib.' He gathered his strength and waved his free hand. 'Getting woozy again, boy. Light … bag of supplies … on back wall …' Then his voice faded. 'Dizzy … can't stay awake. Over to you, son.' He slumped back into unconsciousness.

The old man's breathing was ragged and every now and then he moaned softly. Ellie swallowed hard. Oh God make him all right!

Aaron's hand squeezed her shoulder. 'Don't worry. Sounds like his ankle's twisted, maybe broken, and he's got a cracked rib. That'll hurt like crazy, but it could be worse. We can't do much about that but keep him still. Right now he's better out of it. What's with this light he was talking about?'

Ellie took a deep breath, steadying herself. She remembered Grandpa telling them how he'd kept a lamp and supplies down here ever since he'd been locked in one time. 'Over there, in the corner,' she managed. 'Where Grandpa keeps his cleaning gear. There should be a pressure lamp there.'

The sea seemed quieter now and she heard Aaron move across, banging at boxes and metal containers. Thoughts flashed through her head. Would they ever escape? How had Grandpa got out that other time? Had he forced the hatch? He might be too sick to move now. If he did regain consciousness, what could he do? Could she and Aaron shift the hatch together?

At last Aaron gave a grunt of satisfaction and a match flared in the darkness. 'Here we go,' he muttered and held the flame high. Its momentary glare cut through the blackness, and in that instant Ellie saw a lamp on a wooden shelf above Aaron's head.

'Up there,' she croaked. 'Above your head.'

In a moment, another match flared, the pressure lamp hissed strongly and blessed light flooded the whole dungeon. Aaron lifted the lamp high on to a hook in one corner.

In its glow, the cave looked like the pirate's hide-out in Treasure Island. Strange shadow-shapes flickered in corners, mysterious boxes and mounds of sailing gear loomed against the wall. Aaron squatted down. 'We might be able to use some of this stuff. Be neat if there was something to eat. Hey, cool! Another light.' He held up a torch. 'And look — a tin of bickies and a bottle of water.'

He jiggled the torch beam at Ellie. She glared back at him. Why did boys always have to do that? And how could he even think of food? Beside her, the old man groaned again and Ellie hissed, 'What about Grandpa? What about the first aid stuff?'

Aaron eyed her for a moment, 'Chill out Ellie. I'm working on it. We did first aid in the Outward Bound course last year. I'm trying to remember.' He went on poking through the bag of supplies. 'There's disinfectant, a roll of sticking plaster, aspirin, a knife, rope ...' he fossicked deeper '... a fresh packet of wipes, rags ... pencil and paper.' He reached upwards. 'Then there's this stuff here.' He pulled out two rolls of canvas and an old grey army blanket. 'We should keep your grandpop warm, clean up his cuts and strap up his ankle. It's going to hurt like hell, but it'll be better than nothing.'

'Well do it!' Grandpa said before he slipped sideways so his head fell against Ellie.

She felt the stickiness of blood and stroked him anxiously.

Aaron knelt beside her, carefully examining the cut and the injured ankle. When he took his hand away it also was covered in blood. 'Yeah, well he's got a nasty cut here,' he muttered. 'We can disinfect that and cover it, but I'm afraid his ankle's broken. I'll have to slice his boot off and try and set it.'

'Should I give him an aspirin and a drink?'

'I don't think so.' He frowned. 'If he's got a broken rib, he shouldn't drink anything — just wet his lips. He's not supposed to move.'

The patient groaned, half-conscious now, and muttered, 'Get on with it, boy. Get on with it.'

Gritting his teeth, Aaron cut away the old man's sea boot, exposing a twisted and helpless ankle. As gently as he could, he straightened it and bound the foot tightly into place.

Ellie forced herself to watch. Grandpa was an awful pale colour and he was gripping the rock step so hard his knuckles were white. Sweat and blood ran down his face. She felt sick to her stomach to be so dumb and helpless. She'd never done anything more than patch up Davey's cuts before. But if Aaron could stand it, then so could she.

Just then Aaron glanced up at her set face. 'The head cut's not so bad,' he said. 'Can you fix that up?'

Bracing herself, Ellie wiped the blood from her

grandfather's wound, poured on some disinfectant and covered it with Elastapast. Then she handed him the water bottle. 'Just wet your lips, Grandpa,' she said. 'Slowly. Keep very still and try and rest.'

He glared at her. 'I'm not an invalid!' he muttered, then slid sideways against her again. Ellie's heart lurched with a sudden love and hurt for him. All that growling and barking amounted to zilch. He was as soft as butter underneath. And he'd really done his best for her and Davey. He'd loved them — made them into a proper family with a proper home. Now he was sick and in pain. Ellie felt his pulse like she'd seen Aaron do. It seemed okay — but what did she know?

'Will he be all right?' she murmured as Grandpa drifted off again.

Aaron shrugged. 'As far as I know, he's okay. He's breathing evenly now, but I'd say he'll be out of action for a while.' He glanced up the stone steps. 'He needs help. We just have to get that hatch open. I'll try, but it looks stuck solid. Besides, I think they dumped a weight on it.'

'I heard that too.'

They were right. There was no way the trapdoor would budge.

Ellie cleared her throat, trying to sound cool. 'Your

dad will be able to move it. Davey should be at your place by now. It won't be long.'

Aaron nodded, but he kept his head turned away.

'What's wrong?' she whispered, sensing his doubt. 'They didn't catch Davey, did they?'

He shook his head. 'Not unless they found him afterwards.' He took a deep breath then met her eyes. 'It's just that I remembered Dad left today for Esperance on business. He won't be home until tomorrow. There's no one at our place except ...'

'Your stepmum?'

Aaron nodded again, his face expressionless. 'Yeah — and I'm not even sure about that. She goes out a lot.'

'We-ll,' Ellie shrugged. 'If she's there, she'll do something won't she?'

'I guess so.'

Ellie looked away. Aaron would hate having to say that. He'd hate having to rely on his stepmum — Mrs Freda Wetherington Westway — for help.

She mumbled vaguely, not wanting to explore the idea further, and glanced down. Grandpa needed a doctor. They'd better get help soon. But how? Nobody was even aware anything was wrong. Nobody except Davey. Davey knew — but he didn't know they were stuck down here or anything.

Besides, what could he do? Wait? — or ride to Larsen? In the dark? She gulped, imagining her little brother with no one to turn to, no one to bring help. He'd be so scared ... Ellie swallowed and murmured, 'But your stepmum ... I mean, she'd be back soon after dark, wouldn't she? She must have been expecting you home for tea?'

'If Dad's away I often get my own,' said Aaron shortly.

'Oh,' mumbled Ellie again, unable to add to that. She glanced around the dungeon. Those convicts had been stuck down here for several days. Maybe she, Aaron and Grandpa would be too. Ellie stared uneasily at the iron rings and the place where O.S. Larsen had scratched his initials. None of that was important now. On the other side of the wall the rumble and murmur of the sea seemed quieter.

35

'Ellie,' Aaron squatted down and handed her a biscuit. 'Your grandpop needs a doctor. We've got to do something.'

'Okay. What?'

'Look, maybe Freda'll be home and everything'll be cool. Maybe she'll listen to Davey and get help and everything. But,' he poked the ground uneasily, 'if not, we've got to work out a plan.'

Ellie nodded, munching slowly. 'Davey's the only one who knows anything. If he can't get help he'll come back to the cottage but even he doesn't know we're down here in the dungeon.'

'He'll work it out — or Nibs will. But Nibs and Davey won't be able to open the trapdoor.'

Ellie tried to keep her voice steady. 'There're no phones left working. How'll he get help? He'll be hungry and scared and won't know what to do.' It was how Ellie was feeling herself. And it was getting so cold. Dampness had seeped through her thin sneakers and worked its way up her body. Her jeans were still wet from the struggle on the beach. She shivered, thinking longingly of a hot bath in the big old tub, hot soup and her warm bed.

'Well at least he's got Nibs. And Davey can find himself something to eat.' Aaron half-laughed. 'And it won't be a dry biscuit either.'

Just then a faint uneven rumbling broke through the steady drumming of the sea. They both turned quickly towards the hatch. 'An engine!' squealed Ellie. 'That's an engine!'

Aaron was up the dungeon steps like a shot, pounding on the hatch, shouting, 'We're here! Down here!'

Ellie joined him, banging at the wooden trapdoor, yelling, 'Davey! In the dungeon! We're in the dungeon!' She could hear the motor clearly, idling just the other side of the door. No answer. She raised her voice and bellowed desperately, 'Daveeeeeey! Here! We're down here!' Aaron was yelling too. The engine was cut and she thought she heard a door slam but though they kept yelling, no one answered.

'It's no use,' croaked Aaron. 'They can't hear us.'

'They must!' Ellie was almost weeping. 'We can hear them. Why can't they hear us?' Then above their heads she heard the engine again …. Ellie sank onto the step, sobbing weakly. 'They went! They went! How could they? They didn't even look, they just went!'

Aaron slid down beside her and put his arm around her shoulders. 'They couldn't hear us down here, Ellie — these walls are solid rock.'

'But we could hear them. Why couldn't they hear us?'

'Sounds echo down here, Ellie. They'd be just lost in the open air up there.'

'They didn't even try.' She shook her head from side to side, refusing to believe. 'They could have looked harder. It must have been Davey — he must have come with your step mum. Him and Nibs. Nibs would find us. Why didn't Nibs find us?'

Aaron hunched over and muttered, 'Freda wouldn't bring Nibs in *her* car. She wouldn't take much notice of Davey, either. Probably thought he made it all up.' He thumped one hand slowly with the other. '*And* because everything would be dark, no light in the cottage or anything, she must have decided we weren't here.'

Ellie still couldn't believe it. 'I bet she didn't even

get out of the car,' she repeated dully. 'Not even out of the car.'

Aaron stood suddenly, silent, rigid. Then, turning, he punched the hatch door with all his force. 'Shit!' he shouted. 'Shit! Shit! Shit!' Then he looked down at the open-mouthed Ellie. 'Sorry,' he muttered.

Ellie giggled weakly. 'Cool,' she murmured. 'Shit from me, too.' Then they both laughed — wry, scared, angry — and because it was the only thing to do.

'That's it then,' said Aaron and led the way down the steps.

Ellie struggled to keep the fear out of her voice. She took up her place beside her semi-conscious grandfather. 'You're saying we might be here all night?'

'Yeah, looks like it.' Aaron turned the lamp down. 'The gas won't last either. We'd better save it.'

Ellie felt drained. The thought of a return to complete darkness terrified her. She wanted to cry and plead for Aaron to turn it up but instead she asked, 'How long d'you reckon?'

Aaron shrugged. 'Dunno. We have to expect to wait until morning.' He looked round the room. 'We'd better get as much stuff as we can to wrap ourselves in. Your grandpop'll need to keep warm too. If we huddle up it'll save our body heat.'

Ellie nodded, feeling vaguely embarrassed. She shivered again and murmured, 'I wish the sea would shut up.'

'It sounds worse than it is. The storm was dying when they shoved us in here, and the tide will go out after midnight.'

'Well, right now it sounds to me like the sea could break in any time.'

'Nah. No chance,' Aaron hunched a shoulder and shook his head. 'The rocks've been like this forever. There's a network of caves out there. The waves echo from one to the other; that's why it's so loud all the time.'

'Oh yeah.' He was probably right, but she wasn't going to admit it.

'Look! Solid rock!' He picked up a metal spike and tapped at the rock, stopped, then tapped again. He was wrong! It wasn't solid. It sounded hollow and thin.

Even in the half-light Ellie could see he was surprised. 'Ri-ight,' she scoffed. 'That's solid is it?'

'Sheesh! How about that?' Aaron frowned then shrugged. 'Still, like I said, no big deal, there's no mega flood out there waiting to sweep us off.' He tapped the rock again. 'But I gotta admit it sounds different from what I expected.'

Ellie shrugged and looked away. Different sounds didn't interest her. The sounds she wanted to hear were of human voices and the hatch opening up. But there was only the boom of the sea and Grandpa's occasional soft moan. 'What time is it?' she asked.

Aaron glanced at his watch. 'Eight-forty. Seems later doesn't it?' He stared upwards then muttered, 'Sorry about this.'

'What for? It's not your fault.'

'I sent Davey off. I knew he didn't get on with Freda even if she was home. And I forgot Dad would be out — and,' he banged at the wall again, 'I let myself get caught.'

Ellie rolled her eyes. 'Ohhh, ri-i-ight! That was your fault was it? C'mon, get real. The whole thing was my idea anyway. Nobody's to blame except those crooks. I guess they're way gone by now.'

'Yeah,' Aaron hunched his shoulders. 'The scumbags. I hope they get twenty years.'

'Twenty years is too good for them.'

After a while they had another biscuit and some water. Aaron turned the lamp down to a tiny flame and they curled up either side of Grandpa, pulling the rags and canvas around them. Ellie must have drifted off. Her sleep was full of howling seas, dying seals and a great cold pit. She woke gasping at a falling sensation. Grandpa's arm came round and held her tight. 'It's all right, lassie,' he murmured. 'I've got you. You're safe.'

'Grandpa! You're all right?' She ached all over and her backside was numb.

'Fine, Tiger. Go back to sleep.'

But Ellie sat up. No matter what he said, Grandpa's arm was icy cold and his body was racked with shivers. She shoved his arm under the canvas and felt him wince. He needed a doctor. Worry for the old man swept over her again. She glanced across at Aaron. He was awake too, sitting propped up against the step, staring hard at the back wall. He didn't look as though he'd been asleep at all.

'Obviously no more sign of Davey, or Nibs, eh?' she asked.

'Nah.'

Ellie tried not to sound too anxious. 'I hope he's okay.'

Grandpa gave her a squeeze. 'He's smart enough. He'll be upstairs somewhere, more comfortable than we are.' But Ellie didn't say anything just then about the car that arrived and went away. Grandpa had been unconscious and it seemed just too depressing to go over it all again. He seemed a little better now — or pretended to be. He obviously sensed her mood.

'Time for a snack,' he mumbled. 'Break out the supplies, lad. Then tell me what happened.'

'Not for you, Grandpa,' began Ellie, his cracked rib in mind.

'Rubbish!' He cut her off. 'I'm fine.' But she noticed he didn't eat his biscuit.

While they were munching, Ellie filled the old man in on the struggle with the *Atlantis 3* crew.

'You did well,' he said. 'You couldn't have done anything else.'

Then they did tell him about the car. He grunted and shook his head, shooting a quick glance at Aaron. 'At least Davey's okay. Someone else will arrive in the morning. You sure it was Freda?'

'It sounded like that Triumph Sports of hers,' Aaron muttered. 'She probably saw your truck wasn't there and decided we'd gone with you into town, or Esperance, or the Coastwatch base or wherever.' He shrugged. 'In which case she won't come back here.'

Grandpa eyed the boy keenly. 'So we may not get help for quite a time?'

Aaron nodded reluctantly. 'Unless Davey brings Nibs over tomorrow. If we can get them to hear us, we can send him for help. He can ring from our place.'

'Both our phones were ripped out,' Ellie reminded

her grandfather. 'And Freda — er Mrs Wetherington Westway,' she flushed and didn't look at Aaron, 'may not take much notice of Davey.'

'Ellie's right,' Aaron shifted unhappily and added, 'Dad gets home tomorrow afternoon. He'll listen, he'll come over then.'

Hamish McCleod shifted his position, winced and grunted, 'Well we'll just have to manage as best we can till then, won't we? Don't go blaming yourself, son.'

'But I should've managed better,' grated Aaron. 'If I hadn't let Ellie come, for a start, she'd be free now.'

'As if!' Ellie glared at him. 'Are you mental or something? Then I wouldn't know what happened either. Anyway, how could you stop me, bonehead!'

Aaron mumbled something under his breath. Grandpa chuckled. 'There goes your modern young woman, Aaron old son. I don't know how I would have stopped her either.'

Ellie shrugged. It may be freezing outside, but inside she felt all warm and happy. Grandpa was teasing her. It made her feel closer to him than ever before. 'I suggest sleep, if possible,' he said, and they pulled up the canvas covering once more.

The time dragged by. Ellie eased herself on to the other hip. Cold damp seeped through the old blanket and sailcloth. Every bump in the dungeon floor seemed to be digging in to her body. Maybe she slept but she didn't think so. After a while she gave in and sat up. Beside her, Grandpa stirred and grunted. 'Sleep's a bit impossible, eh?' he snorted dryly. 'Anyone know any good jokes?'

Ellie got up and stamped around humming a tune, trying to get circulation back in her arms and legs. 'You know what Grandpa?' she said. 'You should've put a radio down here. Then we'd have something to listen to.'

'I should leave my mobile down here.'

Ellie turned in surprise, 'What did you say?'

Her grandfather grimaced. 'I was issued with a fancy new gizmo last year.'

Aaron swung round. 'You have a mobile?'

'Yeah,' the old man nodded. 'Of course I do. I've a two-way radio in the ute for when I'm out on patrol — to connect me to Coastwatch. But those thugs will have that. I've got a satellite mobile. It's in my Ranger's kit, in the study. But that's not much use to us at the moment.' Ellie sighed her agreement, and went back to swinging her arms about.

Aaron cleared his throat. 'Those scumbags didn't find it, did they?'

Grandpa frowned. 'They'll find the one in the ute,

and they searched the house. Did they find the one in the study?'

Ellie shook her head. 'It was Hairy-face. He must be pretty dumb. I don't think he found anything. Maybe they'll think the two-way in the ute is all there is. Anyway what use is it to us in the study?'

Aaron spoke again. 'If I could somehow get out, it'd be useful.'

'Like, if we could all get out, it'd be useful,' drawled Ellie.

Aaron ignored her sarcasm. 'Mr McCleod, did you, or Dad and Ellie's mum ever check out down here? For Larsen's Cave, I mean?'

Ellie rolled her eyes. Larsen's Cave? Who cared? Larsen's Cave was a million light years away. Grandpa was lying here hurt, they were trapped in this lousy freezing pit. Forever maybe! Who gave a stuff about a dumb cave? 'What's that got to do with anything?' she croaked.

'Hush, Ellie,' Grandpa frowned at her. 'Of course we checked son. What's your point?'

Aaron went across and tapped the back wall again. 'Well it sounds hollow here, near the carving. I was thinking it might be hollow — a cave — right through to those cliffs under the lighthouse.'

Ellie cut in angrily, 'But it's not important right

now!' From the back of her mind came the sudden memory of that day in the dinghy, and the dark area in the cliff below the lighthouse. She pushed it angrily aside. 'We can't worry about that dumb old cave, now!

'Why not? What else've we got to do?'

Hamish McCleod shifted his position and winced. 'Aaron's right. What else have we got to do?' Then he coughed, winced and asked clearly enough, 'Let's follow your thinking, son.'

Aaron stood up. 'Well, when I knocked that rock wall it was very thin. I mean it sounded hollow.'

'It sounded like the sea could break through,' said Ellie.

'Go on.' The old man's eyes were shut and Ellie could see his pain. He collected his strength and said irritably, 'Go on, lad. Go on.'

'Well,' Aaron took a deep breath, 'maybe there's a network of caves that lead out somewhere. It doesn't have to be Larsen's Cave, of course. But the old maps show there were caves here, way above the waterline at one time.'

'Maybe, but they're below sea level now.'

'I know that,' The boy frowned to hide the eagerness in his voice. 'But it's low tide tonight.'

Hamish opened his eyes. 'You mean we could

knock out a piece of wall and try and escape that way?'

'That's right. So, like I said, we wait for low tide, after midnight then see if we can break through.'

'Then what?'

Aaron grinned. 'Then I take the torch, climb through and see if I can reach the top.' He shrugged, trying to be casual. 'Then I open the hatch, let you out and contact Coastwatch on the mobile so they can send help and catch those scumbags before they get too far.'

'Could be dicey.'

'I reckon I could do it.'

Ellie broke in, 'You're off the planet! The waves'll sweep in here and drown us all.'

'Have you heard any waves for a while?'

No one said anything. Ellie sat still and listened. Almost silence. The sea sounds had dropped to a low murmur. She looked across at her grandfather. His eyes were open and he was staring thoughtfully at Aaron. He didn't believe it surely!

The old man spoke quietly. 'Give the wall a tap again, lad. Let me hear for myself. Aaron got up and walked slowly across the dungeon. Picking up the spike again he tapped the wall.

36

A thin hollow sound echoed round the cavern.

After a while Grandpa said quietly, 'You're right lad. That's thin limestone. A few good strokes and you could break through.'

Ellie swallowed. Grandpa was taking Aaron seriously! He agreed with him! How could he? It was a huge, crazy risk. If the sea rushed back in, it'd fill the dungeon, it'd drown them all! She imagined the dark water pushing them up and up against the hatch until there was no room left, and no air. She cleared her throat and muttered, 'It's a dumb risk, don't you think? I mean what if the sea rushes in?'

Grandpa glanced at her quickly. 'The storm's abated and the tide goes out at midnight, Ellie. Aaron's right. It's at its lowest tonight. It won't be full again until round eight next morning.'

'But it will come in, won't it?' She stared at her grandfather willing him to see the picture of the flooded dungeon that was in her mind. 'What happens then? What happens if Aaron can't reach the top and open the trapdoor?' Her eyes went from one to the other. 'What happens if we're stuck down here?'

Aaron shrugged himself off the wall. 'That won't happen, Ellie.'

They were treating her like an idiot! 'But,' she snapped, 'you don't know that. You don't know what the cliff's like out there. It could be so rough and steep you won't be able to reach anywhere!' She could feel a sob of terror rising in her throat. 'It could be blocked off and then we'll be stuck here and the tide'll come in round eight, and …' her voice started to wobble, 'and we'll drown.'

'Ellie, girl,' Grandpa took both her hands, more patient than she'd ever known him. 'Down here the tide only rises a wee bit — two feet, at most. Not like up north. If it did come in, it'd only wash around the floor a little. If we're still here, we can climb up the steps and be safe.'

'But,' Ellie was unconvinced, 'won't it woooosh in, like a water spout? I've seen the Blow Holes! The water shoots right up in the air.'

Aaron shook his head. 'There's not enough force to push it. The storm's died out and it'll only be low tide anyway.'

Grandpa glanced at the date on his watch. 'Only just lad. One more day left, then it'll be the spring tide. But,' he grinned, 'one day's all we need.'

Ellie rolled her eyes upwards. 'Low tide! Sheesh! How do you know?'

'Tides are pretty regular. They go in cycles. It'll be okay, honest. If I really can't reach the top, I won't take dumb risks. I'll come back and we'll wait for Dad to find us. But if I get out, I can open the hatch, and ring for help to get your grandpop out.'

Hamish McCleod frowned. 'You're not to take risks, son. No risks at all. Not on my account. I'll be fine.' Ellie could see this was a lie. The old man's face was grey and there was blood on his lips where he'd bitten against the pain.

She took a deep breath, embarrassed that she'd sounded such a wuss. 'Okay. Do it.'

Grandpa pulled himself up on one elbow. Ellie could see he was actually excited by Aaron's idea. 'Tools are over there boy. Should be something to do the job.' He dug Ellie in the ribs. 'Turn up the lamp, lass. Give the lad room to swing in.'

Aaron dug out part of an old marlin spike. He

took a few practice swings and grinned. 'Well here goes,' he said, swinging again. Thud! Nothing happened except Aaron yelped, dropped the spike and shook his hands in the air.

'Wrap your hands in rags,' said Grandpa. 'That'll cushion the jarring.'

Aaron wrapped his hands and tried again. He kept it up for about twenty minutes. Chips of rock crumbled and flew off in every direction. A ball of tension built up in Ellie's stomach with every thud. Nothing was happening. She wasn't sure if she wanted it to or not. She wished she hadn't sounded such a wimp, she wished he'd hurry up, that the sea didn't drown them all, that the rest of the cave wasn't about to collapse on top of them. Grit got in her eyes, in her hair. Thud — thud — thud!

Then Aaron was through! A hole the size of a man's fist had appeared in the wall to one side of the carved letters. Icy air whistled through, full of the smell of seaweed and the ocean.

The old man hitched himself on one elbow. 'Well done lad!' he croaked. 'Good work. Open it up.' Over Aaron's head, a few pebbles of limestone broke loose and crumbled away. McCleod glanced upwards. 'Easy. We don't want the whole wall caving in.'

Ellie closed her eyes and swallowed. 'Yeah,' she whispered. 'Why stop now?' Despite her fears, excitement shot through her.

Aaron chipped away. No one tried to talk. Ellie guessed they all felt the same. Escape route it might be, but it could also be a cave beyond a cave, where perhaps long ago Larsen had waited out his last, lonely days. Now they waited here, and like him, nobody knew where they were. Nobody knew enough to come and save them.

'That should do it, boy.' The old man's voice was husky, impatient even. 'Can you see? Can you get through?' Aaron put down the spike and reached for the torch.

'Ellie?' he offered and handed it to her.

37

It was all a bit of an anticlimax, really. The hole Aaron had made was almost in the ceiling of a small cave. The torch beam cut through the blackness and flicked round like a searchlight in an old war movie Ellie had seen once. She pushed down a feeling of disappointment. No skeleton, no treasure, no rusty trunk. Nothing! Just piles of weed and sea rubbish dropped by the tide and banked up on one side. Otherwise the floor and walls were scoured clean. The cave ran seawards, in a series of shadowy arches. Aaron was right. There was a network of caves.

'Well?' Grandpa's voice, impatient, strained, rang out behind her.

She pulled back inside. 'No signs of Larsen or anyone. A whole lot of caves and more caves,' she said. 'No sea at the moment. Looks like you were right, Aaron.' He took the torch from her and went to the opening.

Two spots burned in Grandpa's pale face. He croaked out, 'Nothing else?' He was breathing too fast. Ellie knew it wasn't from excitement.

'I didn't see anything else, Grandpa. But it looks as if Aaron might be able to get through — well, as far as I can see.'

He nodded and with an effort to sound stronger said, 'Better get going boy. Watch your step and come back if it's too bad.' He glared at Aaron. 'You know what to do?'

Aaron pocketed some spare batteries and tied a length of rope round his waist. 'Yes sir. I've been in caves before. I'll stick to the walls.'

The old man nodded. 'Don't tread on any piles of weed. There might be nothing underneath them.' He raised his hand, eyes half-closed with pain. 'Good luck son.'

Aaron grinned nervously and flicked his fingers at Ellie. 'See ya,' he mumbled.

'Yeah, right.' She was scared, not wanting him to go. 'Watch out for creatures from the black lagoon.' He grinned again and disappeared through the hole.

Time dragged. Ellie checked Grandpa's bandagings and snuggled up beside him. Every now and then he shivered and seemed to fall into a drowsy unconsciousness that was almost worse than before. At least now, if Aaron got through they could get help on the mobile. She wished he'd hurry — Grandpa needed warmth and proper treatment. He was in bad pain and she wasn't sure how much more he could stand.

After a while he woke and sipped a little water from the bottle. Ellie could feel his rapid heartbeat as she lay against him. She wished she knew what to do.

He must have read her mind because his hand squeezed her shoulder. 'I'm a tough old coot. I'll be fine.'

'You shouldn't talk, Grandpa. Save your strength.'

He snorted dryly. 'They always say that on television, don't they? Well,' he grunted and changed position, 'I want you to talk to me. Keep my mind off my aches and pains.' So sometimes they talked, and sometimes they didn't. They talked about Ellie's mum, and Shelley, about Davey, and what Ellie wanted to do with her life, and a whole lot of other things. Grandpa forgot to be growly and Ellie knew she'd always remember this as a special time. But she could see the old man was getting tired.

'Aaron would have been back by now if he

couldn't get through,' she tried to sound positive. 'You should rest awhile and gather your strength so we can get you out of here.'

He ruffled her hair. 'I intend to be conscious and ready when that young fella opens the hatch.'

'You believe he'll make it, Grandpa?'

'I do. He's a smart young bloke. If he's got his sights set on something, he'll do it.'

'D'you think we've found Larsen's Cave?'

'How do I know girlie? Nothing much in that cave, you said.'

'No, but I only had a quick look. The sea seems to have washed everything clean.'

'Well, it's had over two hundred and fifty years to do it. There won't be much to find even if that was Larsen's Cave, poor devil — the waves have been in and out of there for too long.'

Ellie buried her head into Grandpa's chest. 'It'd be so bad dying all alone like that, with no one — not his family, not his friends, not anyone — even knowing where he was. We've had that feeling for just a few hours. He had it for a lifetime.' They fell silent.

Grandpa fumbled for her hand and patted it. 'We don't know he was all alone. He may have had friends among the Aborigines.'

'You said they told you he kept to himself.'

'Yes, well — who knows? Life plays funny tricks. I was all alone until you and Davey turned up.' He squeezed her hand. 'Now I've got a family.'

Ellie squeezed his hand back. 'And we've got you,' she whispered, and fell silent, thinking about Mum and how, because she'd been killed, they'd come to Grandpa and Lighthouse Cottage. It was a pretty awful way to find a family. She sighed.

The old man pulled her close to him. He guessed what she was thinking.

'She'd be proud of you, lass. So am I. You and young Davey have got me going again.' He snorted with amusement. 'What the Welfare lady would call "a positive learning experience," I think,' he ruffled her hair. 'Mags'd be glad for all of us.'

'I reckon she would, too,' murmured Ellie, refusing to allow tears. 'I love Lighthouse Cottage. So does Davey.'

'Except,' Grandpa eased his leg into a new position, 'we seem to have misplaced that young scamp somewhere.'

Ellie sat up. 'Well,' she grinned, 'if he's with Mrs Freda Wetherington Westway, it'll be a real learning experience for both of them.'

He gave a husky laugh, then winced. 'Be worth seeing.'

Just at that moment they heard a shout and the grating sound of something being dragged above the trapdoor. A gust of air surged in as it opened, and a torch, followed by Aaron's face, appeared in the opening.

'How's it going down there?' he called. 'I made it! Here comes the relief team.'

38

After that everything happened quickly. Contact with Coastwatch brought promise of an ambulance, a doctor and a search for *Atlantis 3*.

Ellie watched the headlights of the ambulance roaring up the track, emergency light flashing, siren wailing. She knew Grandpa would hate all the fuss, but she thought flashing lights and sirens were great — right at this moment anyway. Grandpa would be okay now, at least she hoped so.

The ambulance men carried him up from the dungeon on a stretcher. The young doctor examined him quickly and ordered him, despite protests, to hospital in Esperance. 'That's a nasty break, Mr McCleod,' he said. 'You're probably concussed and in shock. The kids did okay for you, but we have to clean that head wound properly and set that ankle or you'll be hobbling around for the rest of your life.'

'That's all very well,' grumbled the old man. 'All this hullaballoo. But what about the kids?'

'Don't fuss Grandpa,' Ellie whispered. 'The Coastwatch man is here and it'll be light in a few hours. Then I'll find Davey and sort things out. We'll be okay. You just do as you're told and let the doctor get you better quick!'

'And what then?' He was fighting pain and exhaustion.

'I'll get Dad to come over, Mr McCleod,' said Aaron. 'He can stay with us until you get back. He knows what to do round the lighthouse and we can help.'

Hamish McCleod opened his eyes, stared at the boy, and nodded. 'Let me know.'

The stretcher was strapped in and the ambulance was ready to leave. 'You kids sure you'll be okay?' asked the driver. 'Mac from Coastwatch is going to be pretty busy. You can come into town with us and we'll find you a bed.'

'No thanks,' said Ellie. 'We've got someone coming.' She hoped that was true. 'and we'll get Aaron's dad to bring us to the hospital later.' She swallowed and asked, 'Will Grandpa be okay?'

'He'll need a cast,' the doctor told her. 'As long as there's no infection or other complications, he should be home in a week.'

Ellie nodded. 'Just get him better,' she implored. As the ambulance rumbled up the track, Ellie prayed that whoever looked after grandfathers would care for this one very carefully.

Inside the cottage Ellie handed Aaron a towel and showed him how to work the ancient heater above the bath tub. 'You first,' she told him. 'Don't use all the hot water. I'll get us some soup.'

An hour later, warm, fed, and surprisingly wide awake, Aaron and Ellie sat at the kitchen table. Down on Our Beach a Coastwatch officer was checking out the dinghy from *Atlantis 3*.

'It'll be light soon,' she said. 'I reckon Davey'll turn up when he can see to find the way.'

Aaron nodded. 'He won't hang around my place any longer than he has to, that's for sure.' His finger circled a mark on the scrubbed pine table. 'Poor little dude, he'll be worried sick.'

Ellie grinned. 'He'll survive. I don't think our Davey's much of a worrier. Grandpa said he'd like to see your stepmum and Davey sort each other out.'

Aaron grunted with amusement. 'Yeah.' He wet his finger and dabbed at the crumbs on the plate. Something was on his mind.

'You want any more?'

'Nah, thanks. I keep thinking of everything.'

Ellie watched him. This was a very different Aaron from the one she'd first met, but she was beginning to know his moods. You didn't have to be brilliant to guess what this 'everything' was about. 'What're they like?' she asked, 'the caves?'

He flashed a grin at her. 'Huge! It's a whole gallery down there.' Excitement fizzed from him. 'And that one we broke through — that's just the bottom section of a massive network! It's like Wow! Really major.'

'That major, eh?'

'Fully mega major!' He glanced up quickly. 'You tired?'

Ellie shook her head. 'Nah.'

'Me neither.' He was quiet for a moment and circled the mark on the table again. 'Those caves are really something.'

Ellie stared at him, reading his mind. Sheesh! He wanted to go back into the dungeon again. 'You're not serious? You don't want to go back down there?'

He looked up and grinned. 'Don't you? But if we don't go now, we'll have to wait 'til the weather improves. The spring tide is due, and,' he pointed to the barometer, 'another low is coming through. It wouldn't be safe. I don't reckon I can wait that long.'

'You must be brain-dead!'

'Probably, but think about it. If we wait, by the time we can explore down there we'll have to share it with everyone. Before that, it'd be really neat to see if we can find Larsen's Cave on our own.'

Ellie's finger took over the mark on the table. 'You really reckon it's there?'

Aaron flicked back a strand of hair and his eyes gleamed. 'It's the coolest bet so far.'

'I guess you're right,' Ellie nodded slowly. 'You know, I should have thought of it before. I noticed a sort of dark break in the cliff from the dinghy one day. But it looked all under water.'

'The entrance and lower tunnel would be at high tide.'

'Grandpa asked us not to do dumb things. I sort of promised ...' her voice trailed off.

Aaron nodded, 'Yeah well, we won't be stupid or anything.' He glanced at his watch. 'It's nearly daylight. If we wait till Davey comes, we could get him to stay up and keep the hatch open. Would you come then?'

'Will the tide be out?'

'Until eight — and it comes in low and slowly.'

Ellie didn't say anything for quite a while. Then she nodded. 'Okay,' she said. 'If you promise we'll be back before eight.'

Aaron shrugged. 'Cool,' he said.

Davey arrived on his bike an hour later. They heard Nibs barking on the hill above the cottage, and Aaron and Ellie went out into the courtyard. Nibs got there first, wriggling round their legs, bouncing up to try and lick their faces. Davey didn't even pause, he dropped his bike and ran headfirst into his sister, arms around her, fists thumping. 'Where were you? Where were you? You didn't stay. I thought the scumbags had you. I told her and told her. She wouldn't let me come!' Words bubbled out of him as tears ran down his cheeks. He took a breath and looked up. 'Ellie? Where were you? That old bag ...' He stopped and glanced quickly at Aaron. 'That Mrs Wether Westwhat, she said you'd gone, that Grandpa'd gone too and you'd left me.' He pounded her again. 'You did leave me.'

Ellie dodged his flailing fists and hugged her little brother. 'The scumbags did get us Davey. They locked us in the dungeon, and ...'

His eyes rounded. 'In the dungeon? In Grandpa's dungeon? Where is Grandpa?' He stared frantically. 'Where is Grandpa?' Gradually he calmed down as Ellie told him the whole story.

'But I didn't find you,' he gulped. 'We came in the

car but,' he didn't look at Aaron this time, 'she wouldn't let me look for you.'

'You couldn't hear us shouting, Davey. You wouldn't hear anything coming from the dungeon.'

'But it's so awful down there, and,' he looked up, eyes full of tears, 'Grandpa is hurt. He's in hospital. Mum went to hospital and she ...'

'He's going to be okay, Davey,' Ellie held him to her. 'He's just got a broken ankle, like Mr Wiley had once, remember. Grandpa's okay. He'll be home in a week or so.'

Aaron patted his arm. 'Ellie's right, mate. Dad'll come over here. I'll stay too and we'll all look after the lighthouse and cottage till your grandpop gets back.'

Davey rubbed at tears and a dripping nose. 'We'll be lighthouse keepers? Real lighthouse keepers?'

'Like Grandpa, Davey.'

He sniffed noisily and stared at them for a minute. 'Okay.' His voice was husky. 'And we'll look after the lighthouse, and the cottage, and the envir ...' he struggled with the word, 'evirment ... and Grandpa, when he comes home?'

'That's right mate. And your grandpop'll be fine in no time.' Aaron stood. 'You had breakfast?'

Davey shook his head. 'Naa. I just grabbed an apple and snuck off.'

'C'mon then,' said Ellie. 'I'll get you some. Then there's something we want to talk to you about.'

Davey sat at the kitchen table, swinging his legs and munching a Vegemite sandwich. He was working out the whole story in his head. Finally he asked, 'How *did* you get out of the dungeon?' Aaron told him.

'You found the cave?' His wide eyes moved from one to the other. 'You found Mr Larsen's Cave?' Davey was never quite sure if they were talking about Mr Olaf Larsen from the general store, or someone else. He didn't much care. If you're looking for a cave, you're looking for a cave.

'We don't know yet, Davey,' said Ellie. 'But we want to go and have another look, before the tide comes in.'

The little boy swallowed. 'Go down there, you mean? Down in the dungeon? But you just got out.'

'Yeah,' Aaron picked at the mark on the kitchen table. 'Yeah we were sort of hoping you'd stay by the hatch and watch out for us, Davey.'

'I don't have to go down there?' There was relief in his voice.

'No,' Ellie shook her head. 'Just make sure the hatch door doesn't shut and get help if we need it. Okay?'

'Okay,' said Davey happily. 'I'll tie it down and sit on the rope. Nibs and me'll sit on it.' He frowned. 'But you be careful, Ellie,' he swallowed anxiously. 'Don't you get hurt, too.'

'It'll be cool,' said Ellie firmly, and prayed she was right.

39

Loaded with torches, another pressure lamp, extra batteries, candles and a roll of rope, Aaron and Ellie climbed back down into the dungeon.

'We'll light the lamp and leave it here,' said Aaron. 'That way we'll see the glow to find the way back.'

Ellie swallowed uneasily. She wasn't planning to go far from the dungeon. She glanced at her watch. Six-twenty. There should be plenty of time before the tide came in. Okay,' she murmured. 'Let's go for it.'

Aaron led the way, wriggling through the hole and dropping to the floor of the cave below. Ellie followed him. He swung the powerful torch beam round the whole cavern then held it steady in one direction. 'That's the way out,' he said, his voice echoing back at them. 'It's easy. Just spills out into a little cove. But that,' he swung the torch the other way, 'is where we ought to look first.'

Ellie gasped. He was right about it being huge! Tier upon tier of rock ledges stretched back into the distance, each one a little higher than the last. Every now and then there was a dark opening, perhaps to another opening off the main gallery. 'Wow!' she whispered. 'It's like … like an office building, an art gallery — room after room!'

Aaron nodded. 'Now,' he grinned. 'If you were Mr O. S. Shipwrecked Larsen, or whoever, where would you start looking for ace accommodation? C'mon!'

'What about the tide?' Anxiety made Ellie's voice extra loud. It repeated back to her, over and over, '… the tide … the tide …'

'Those far ledges are way above any tide line. They'd be as high as the cottage. Maybe a tad noisy in a storm though.' Aaron flicked a pebble into the darkness. It was only a small pebble but it sent echoes cascading through the cavern. Ellie could imagine how waves would boom in a storm.

As they climbed the ledges the rock got drier and drier. On and on they went, further and further, until it seemed to Ellie they must be deep inside the earth. Driftwood and shells piled up in banks and corners. Now and then they came upon the skeleton of a small creature. Ellie guessed they were mostly rat skeletons, but she didn't ask. Looking back, there was no sign of the glow from the pressure lamp in the dungeon. 'How far are we going?' she murmured.

Aaron came back. 'What d'you reckon?'

'Not much further. The dungeon's quite a way back down there.' She didn't want to sound like a wuss but she couldn't help adding, 'This looks as though it goes on forever. It'd be easy to lose your way. The tide comes in at eight, remember?'

Aaron nodded and glanced at his watch. 'An hour to go. We don't have to do it all today, but there's another cave coming up. How about we check that out and then go back?'

Ellie nodded and led the way up a natural rock stairway into a cavern. Suddenly she stopped, speechless. She struggled to find words. Finally she managed, 'It's here! Aaron it's here! We've found it! Larsen's Cave! This is it. We've found Larsen's Cave!'

Ellie heard Aaron's indrawn breath behind her as his torch joined hers and swept the cavern. Figures and faces reared out at them, distorted in the half-light. A chill slid down Ellie's back and she bit back a small scream.

'It's cool, Ellie. Stay there.' Aaron's hand patted her shoulder, then he bent and stuck four lighted candles in the clean dry sand of the floor. The glow brought the whole room alive! Each wall was covered in a pageant in stone — men, women, animals — every shape and form imaginable was outlined in hardened limestone. Aaron and Ellie stepped back, mouths open, words lost.

Aaron found his voice first. 'Unbelievable!' he gasped. 'It must be his story — Larsens' story.' There could be no doubt. The walls were covered with etchings of ships, animals, people — there was even a map of sorts. Some of the people wore horned helmets, like Vikings. Every now and then there were words in a strange language!

'It must have taken him forever,' breathed Ellie.

'Yeah, the rest of his life.'

They circled the cave slowly, taking in the carvings, working out their meaning. 'That's the storm,' muttered Ellie. There was no mistake. The masts of a ship stuck out at an angle from a broken craft, lines of waves and tossing sea smashed at its hull, despairing faces sank through the water.

Aaron shook his head in disbelief. 'He was so good, really good. Lots of sailors carved things, but he must have been an artist, or something.'

'Grandpa told me the Aborigines talked about him carving rocks and wood. This is what they meant.'

'Look!' Aaron pointed at the map. 'That's Europe and the Mediterranean! And there's Africa. Look and here's the coast near Cape Leeuwin. He's carved his journey! His whole story's here!'

The face of an Aboriginal man stared out over a hunting scene of men with spears and a kangaroo. In the background mia mias huddled along the edge of a creek. A life-size Aboriginal woman leaned gracefully against the stump of a tree, the detail of face and hands perfect.

'Perhaps she was his friend,' murmured Ellie and hoped she was right. Beside the woman was another kangaroo. It could almost have been alive. And there was a strange striped, dingo-like creature with a rigid tail.

Aaron squatted down. 'I think that's a thylacine.' He stared around. 'Nothing like this has been found in Australia before, ever. It's massive! Huge! And it's so well preserved! I still can't believe it.' Ellie nodded. She felt stunned. It was almost too much to take in. She stared round the rest of the cave. There was a ledge, higher than the others with a niche carved in the side. Perhaps he slept there. She went over to investigate. There was something there!

'Aaron,' she gasped. 'Look! There's a box or something up there. That must have been his bed.

He must have slept there and ...' she swallowed. She didn't want to say that he must have died there.

Aaron lifted down a small box folded in oilskin. As he unwrapped it, the lid came into view, the metal moulded to show a ship in full sail. Brass sea dragons formed the hinges. He ran his hands over the mouldings and looked up at Ellie. 'Shall I open it?'

She nodded. 'Be careful. It may be fragile.'

Aaron gently worked at the catch with his pocket knife, scraping at the built-up rust. 'It's coming,' he murmured and lifted the lid.

Inside was a crucifix on a string of black carved stones, and a tiny package wrapped in finer oilskins. 'A rosary,' Ellie lifted the beads. 'A few kids at Shelley had them. It's kind of a special gift that you get on your first communion or something. This must have been special to Larsen.'

Aaron nodded. 'Yeah. He kept it in the safest place.' He picked up the tiny package. 'This one is pretty fragile. I don't want to tear it or anything. We'll open it later.' They both fell silent, letting the magic of Larsen's work sweep over them again.

Ellie didn't know what she'd expected to find. When she'd thought of the cave, she'd imagined parts of a ship, fittings, pewter mugs, a skull, bones, maybe a chest with the crumbling skeleton of Larsen propped against it. Certainly nothing like this. Here was no treasure, no skeleton, no brass-bound chest of doubloons. Here, instead, was a simple rosary and a tiny package. And everywhere were the dreams and memories of that lonely Swedish sailor who'd carved from his soul two hundred and fifty years ago. She took a shaky breath. This was so much better; this was like getting to know Larsen.

Ellie glanced at Aaron. He had the same look of wonder on his face that she was feeling. He caught her look and smiled. 'It's brilliant. Just right.'

They retraced their steps round the cavern, examining the detail in every carving. Suddenly Aaron glanced at his watch. 'God! It's twenty to eight! The tide will start flowing in twenty minutes.'

Ellie swallowed and shivered. She'd forgotten the time. 'How long will it take us to get back?'

Aaron looked at his watch again. 'We'd better move. In fact, we'd better run!' He shoved the metal box into the chest pocket of his anorak and they started to run.

40

To Ellie, it seemed harder going down than up. Their downward scramble over the bumps and hollows of the ledges made it difficult to balance. Twice she fell, but the thought of the tide sweeping back into the cave was enough to keep her going.

She paused to catch her breath and Aaron hurried her on. 'Halfway to go yet, Ellie. C'mon.' She pushed herself off and pounded after him. Down, down they ran, on and on, the lights of their torches flicking crazily across ceiling and wall.

They rounded the last gallery into ankle-deep water. The torch-beams picked out the steadily rising sea, moving across the tunnel floor. A sudden swoosh sent it surging round Ellie's legs. 'I thought you said it didn't woosh in,' she panted.

Aaron didn't stop to argue. 'We're nearly there. Keep going.'

They splashed on.

Ellie never thought she'd be so glad to see the dungeon. Aaron made a stirrup of his hands and heaved her up to the opening. She wriggled through and turned to help him, then they tumbled backwards to fall giggling and panting on the dungeon floor.

'Wow,' gasped Ellie. 'You said the tide only rose half a metre!'

Aaron shrugged. 'Half a metre of moving water is like ...' he made a face, 'half a metre of moving water — quite big. But,' he grinned, 'it's not going to come wooshing in here and drown us. It might wash up the ledges a bit.' He sat up and pulled the metal box from his anorak. 'But heh! Was that worth it, or what?'

Ellie caught her breath. 'Huge! Something else! So huge I can't believe it.' She shook her head, then sighed. 'I guess it's pretty valuable, huh? People will have to know.'

Aaron rolled his eyes. 'Mega, mega priceless. Not just money-priceless but what it means — the history and stuff! We won't be able to keep this secret. Larsen's Point will make world headlines. The whole world will know about it. There'll be experts and history dudes all over the place.' He grimaced. 'But we found it first, Ellie. You and me ...'

Ellie stared back through her mind. '... And Mum, and your dad, Grandpa — even Davey. They've all been part of the looking.' She suddenly felt weepy. 'Mum would have spun out of her head if she'd seen it. She was so keen on ...'

'Ellie!' It was Davey. 'Is that you Ellie?' He sounded scared. Nibs was barking.

'It's okay, Davey. We're back.' She got up and started to climb the steps. 'C'mon Aaron, we can look at the box in the kitchen.'

'You were ages!' Davey accused them. 'Nibs was scared.'

Aaron climbed out and closed the hatch. 'You did a good job standing guard, little mate. We found Larsen's Cave, and stacks of others. One day I'll show you.'

'Grandpa too?' said Davey. He still didn't fancy the dungeon, but the thought of stacks of caves was hard to resist.

'Only with Grandpa,' said Ellie firmly.

In the kitchen, Aaron slipped the catch on the metal box and carefully placed the rosary and the oilskin package on the table. 'You open it,' he said to Ellie. She picked up the parcel wonderingly. It had been like that for two hundred and fifty years. No one but Aaron and herself had touched it since. Her fingers felt stiff and clumsy. She peeled the oilskin back slowly, feeling it hard and brittle in her hands. Gradually the folds cracked open. Inside was a small book, its cover black and mouldy with age, the edges flaking on the corners.

'It's only a book,' snorted Davey. 'A church book.' He picked up the black-beaded crucifix and his nose wrinkled in disgust. 'Timmy Riley had a church book and one of these necklace things in Shelley.'

'Not like this, he didn't,' murmured Ellie. Gently she lifted the cover of the book and peered at the water-stained pages. They were thin and yellowed but the markings were quite clear. 'Davey's right,' she said. 'It's a miniature Bible. I can't read the language, but it's got a picture of an angel with a sword and Bible sort of printing.'

Aaron took it from her hands and turned the flyleaf. Someone had written on the blank first page. The writing was tiny, wobbly and the letters strangely formed, but the word 'Larsen' stood out clearly enough.

'It was his,' whispered Ellie. 'His Bible. He must have saved it from the wreck and kept it with him all that time. It must have reminded him of home and everything. I wonder what the writing says?'

'Well,' said Aaron. 'I guess it's Swedish.' He

raised his eyebrows. 'Old Mr Larsen'll go ape.'

'Will he come and live in his cave?' asked Davey happily. 'I like Mr Larsen.'

'Wrong Larsen, Davey,' said Ellie. 'But I bet he claims he's related. Anyway,' she picked up the Bible, 'I guess he'll be able to tell us what this says.'

41

Later that morning, Michael Westway arrived. 'Freda got a message to me,' he said, getting out of the Jeep. 'How did Davey end up at our place last night? What's happened here, and where's Hamish?'

'In hospital,' said Ellie, leading the way inside.

'My God! What on earth's been going on? Is he okay?'

'Grandpa's got a broken ankle like Mr Wiley,' said Davey. 'He's gone to hospital.' He leaned into Ellie frowning hard. 'But he's not going to die.'

Ellie pushed aside her worries. 'He's in shock and in bad pain, but the doctor reckons he'll be home in a week.'

Aaron scowled. 'The scumbags really beat him up.'

His father limped in and sat heavily on a kitchen chair. 'You'd better start the whole story from the beginning,' he said. 'It sounds like all hell broke loose over here, last night.'

It took some time for Michael Westway to sort out the various strands of the story. When it was all done he shook his head. 'Amazing! Absolutely bloody amazing! And you're not hurt, any of you?'

'Just Grandpa.'

Michael Westway blew out a long stream of air and grinned. 'I bet he gives them ginger in hospital. We'll have to spell the nurses. Now,' he took a deep breath, 'I want to hear all about Larsen's Cave.'

'It's unbelievable,' muttered Aaron. He described it — the tiers and tiers of ledges like a gallery and the final cavern, all the carvings. 'Even some Vikings, Dad. It looked like a legend or something. The guy was brilliant.'

Aaron didn't say anything about his and Ellie's race against the incoming tide.

Ellie wasn't going to either. 'Mr Larsen's whole journey's there,' she said. 'A map — everything, Aborigines, a beautiful lady, and animals, even what Aaron thinks is a thylacine.'

'Good lord. They've been extinct since the 1930s. It must be breathtaking. I suppose it's too late for me to …'

'The tide's in, Dad. The spring's due and another

low. You could be caught.' He flushed. 'It's quite a way.'

Michael Westway sighed. 'I guess you're right. I'll just have to wait and take it slowly.'

He bent forward and gave Ellie and Davey a clumsy hug. 'Your mum and I searched and searched for that damn cave, you know. I started to doubt it ever existed, but she never did.'

Ellie nodded. 'I know,' she whispered. 'But we used your notes and maps while we looked. So ...' she blew her nose, 'we reckon you and Mum, Grandpa and Davey all helped find the cave too.'

Aaron's dad picked up the small Bible. 'What d'you want to do with this?'

'Can you look after it for a while?' asked Ellie. 'We want to show it to Mr Larsen. Before everyone finds out about the cave and everything, we want Mr Larsen to translate the handwriting for us. And we want to wait for Grandpa.'

That afternoon they went in to see Hamish. He glared at them over the top of his hospital sheet while the nurse fussed with a support sling for his ankle. 'A fine thing, this is,' he muttered. 'Trussed up here like a damn cocky on a perch. Well, where've you all been? What's happened? What've you found?'

'Oh boy,' sighed Ellie, and told him. '… and,' she finished, 'Coastwatch have busted those scumbags from *Atlantis 3*. I hope they stick them away for life.'

By the end of the week Grandpa was ready to come home and the hospital was happy to let him go. A solid cast encased his ankle. He had a crutch for support, and he used it like a weapon, directing orders, poking anyone unlucky enough to get in his way.

Ellie settled him into a chair on the verandah. 'We've asked Olaf Larsen over to look at the Bible, rosary and stuff,' she said.

'Huh! The big clown'll claim they belonged to his great-great-great-uncle or someone,' grumbled Grandpa. 'He'll make a fortune out of it … spin a tale for all the tourists … turn out in a Viking's helmet and sell copies of his family tree at the general store.'

'Grandpa,' Ellie shook her head at him. 'Be nice, okay?'

He grinned at her. 'Well, when is Olaf, the Viking avenger, getting here?'

Olaf arrived before lunch. Davey had lost interest in the Bible and was ready to go fishing, but there were no takers. He leaned up against the big Swede, hoping to change his mind, but Olaf could hardly wait to play his part. He smiled a gappy smile and the points of his beard twitched. 'Such a day,' he sighed. 'Such a day.'

Sitting at the kitchen table, Olaf picked up the small metal box in his big hands. Gently he took out the beads and opened the tiny Bible. Tears ran down his face. 'Two hundred and fifty years!' he sobbed. 'And now ve find him, now ve know him. Now Olaf Sven Larsen come back to us.'

'Olaf Sven?' asked Aaron. 'How d'you know it's Olaf Sven?'

'I just know,' announced Olaf, loftily. 'Besides, it says so. Now everyone shush!' He settled his spectacles, cleared his throat and began to read. '*This Holy Book be given to Olaf Sven Larsen by his mother Elka Larsen Johansen. It be his father's, and his father's before that. May God have Mercy.*' He stopped.

'Is that all?' whispered Ellie.

'There is more,' said Olaf sternly. 'Yah. He writes: *On this day I join my Father, and his father. I pray my soul vill leave this vild land and go home. I have lived, I have sung, I have told my life, and now I die. God have mercy.* That is all.' The big Swede wiped his eyes again. 'He talks of singing his story.' That is what a Viking does — sings his story.'

Ellie knew what he meant. Grandpa had told her how in the old times, when a Viking warrior died, his people sang the story of his life. That way his story lived on from one generation to another. She repeated the last words in Larsen's Bible: *I have sung, I have told my life, and now I die. God have Mercy.*

Nobody spoke for a while. Then Grandpa murmured, 'God have mercy.' Ellie whispered it too. It was like a prayer.

42

It was a month before it was safe enough for them all to return to Larsen's Cave. Grandpa raged and snapped over the delay. Finally, with his ankle strapped firmly and Ellie supporting one elbow, he and Mike Westway hobbled eagerly through the tiers of caverns until they stood in the small cave.

Olaf held the lamp high and the scenes on its walls came to life. Once again the ship tossed and sank in cruel seas, men drowned, and on the shore families and animals went about their daily tasks. The thylacine hunted the kangaroo, ducks swam in a creek and the beautiful woman, leaning against the stump of the tree, looked out on a kindly land.

'My God!' wondered Hamish McCleod. 'It's a sort of miracle. Like a tapestry in stone.' Michael Westway traced the map of Larsen's journey with the same wonder on his face that Ellie had seen on Aaron's.

Olaf wept again. 'It is a great singing,' he sobbed. 'Like the old times — a Viking has sung his life.'

And the song was there in front of them. Larsen's story, carved so far away from his homeland, would last forever. Ellie took a deep breath. It was strange to feel so close to someone who had lived and died over two hundred years ago. She stared again at the amazing story around her. To be lost as well as lonely would be the hardest thing. Larsen had been lost for half a lifetime, yet he'd brought to life all the people he knew — right up to the Aboriginal friends who'd saved his life. Maybe he wasn't as lonely as she'd first thought. He seemed to have managed okay — well, she could too. After all, she'd only been lost for a little while, and she had Davey and Grandpa, and ... she looked across the cavern ... and Aaron, and everyone else.

Aaron caught her eye and smiled. 'This is how we talked, isn't it Ellie,' he said. 'O.S. Larsen is really somebody now. And the guy's even cooler than we thought. He didn't just sit around waiting, doing nothing. He told us who he is and what he did. He wasn't just going to vanish off the face of the earth.'

'In fact,' his father murmured. 'You could say he really did put Larsen's Point on the map.'

Davey huddled up close to Grandpa. 'Let's go,' he muttered. 'This place is full up.'

Acknowledgements

Thanks to Val who helped me write this through the dark times, and to Alwyn and Fremantle Arts Centre Press for their guidance and support.